# Lincoln and Kansas
## Partnership for Freedom

ABRAHAM LINCOLN
L. Prang & C. Boston

*If I went West, I think
I would go to Kansas . . .* A. Lincoln

# Lincoln and Kansas
## Partnership for Freedom

by
*Carol Dark Ayres*

*Best Wishes to client
and Billy Jean.*

*Carol Dark Ayres*

**Sunflower University Press**®

1531 Yuma • P.O. Box 1009 • Manhattan, Kansas 66505-1009 USA

Cover: From the Saint Mary College Collection, Leavenworth, Kansas.
Photography by Jeffrey A. Borbely.

ISBN 0-89745-254-2

Sunflower University Press is a wholly-owned subsidiary
of the non-profit 501(c)3 Journal of the West, Inc.

*For my mother,*
*Wilma Dark*

# Contents

# Preface

*T*HE MARK OF A great man, it has been said, is that the more you know about him the more you like him. This has certainly been true of my journey with Abraham Lincoln; the more I learned about him, the more I respected and admired him. In January 1997, I became the Special Collections Librarian at Saint Mary College, Leavenworth, Kansas. A part of my responsibility was the Abraham Lincoln Collection. The first step to knowing the Collection was to understand Lincoln, the man. That was the beginning of an ongoing journey that may never end, as there is so much written about him.

Saint Mary College was given the Lincoln Collection because of his visit to Kansas in 1859. I gradually became aware of the importance of Kansas in the whole drama of Lincoln and the issue of slavery, and, yet, there was very little written about his Kansas visit.

My determination grew to let Kansans know of their part in this important historical event. I originally had planned to write a pamphlet, as surely there couldn't be too much information concerning one short week. This brochure would be given to visitors to our collection and to other historical institutions that might want to share such information. Well, I researched, and my "pamphlet" grew larger and larger, until finally it was more like a book.

As I read the original documents, the language of the time was so colorful and expressive that I decided I must share this with the reader. Early on, I resolved that this book would be, as closely as possible, a first-hand observation of that week in Kansas history. I wanted the reader to experience the original newspaper articles and reports and know the event for themselves, not filtered through my eyes and mind or summarized by me. Therefore, I determined that I would include, in full, every newspaper article, letter, and report of the event. Of course, some memoirs were too long and I had to summarize, but overall I stuck to my original plan. I also wanted this work to be a complete report of everything that was written about the event so that historians or others who wanted to know something about Lincoln's visit to Kansas could find it all in one place. Original documents are left as they were written — no misspelled words are changed and, in an effort to enhance the reading, explanatory [*sic*] markings have been omitted.

Quickly, I learned just how much mythology and lore have grown to surround Abraham Lincoln over the years. It seems that Lincoln had slept in every home and hotel in the area. Searching through the many conflicting stories and reports was interesting, but also, at times, frustrating. Trying to find the historical facts among the fiction was a challenge. I was anxious to include every wonderful story, but also determined to confirm the historical veracity. Because some tales that I could not confirm were just too good to be left out, I have called them stories or folklore. They could very well be true, and I hope they are.

I share with Abe Lincoln his love of stories. As he said, "A good story is medicine to my bones." Thus, I have tried to tell the story of Lincoln's visit to Kansas and hope that it is, indeed, medicine to the bones.

Everyone with whom I have come in contact and asked for help was so eager and cooperative that it was a pleasure to work on the book.

Librarians from as far away as New York City and Washington, D.C., have willingly researched and sent me copies of original sources that were very important to this work. Rodney O. Davis, of the Lincoln Studies Center, Knox College, Galesburg, Illinois, graciously read the work. I especially need to thank Lieutenant General Robert Arter, who is a benefactor to the Collection and has been an enabler and encourager, as well as the catalyst, not only for this book, but for many possibilities for the Collection. I also owe a debt of gratitude to Johnny Johnston, in essence also a writer, who was the originator of the idea of preparing a pamphlet about the history of the Collection and Lincoln's visit. And, finally, a special thank you to Sandra Borbely who has been my assistant researcher, editor, and overall helper in this project; I couldn't have done it without her.

I am grateful that my life has been so much enriched by all of the people with whom I have met and worked during this project. I am also grateful to the early people of Kansas and the sacrifices they made in our behalf, and, of course, I am grateful most of all, as are all Americans, to the Great Emancipator, Abraham Lincoln.

Abraham Lincoln.
*Kansas State Historical Society, Topeka*

*Chapter One*

# Kansas Territory and Its People

HE STORY OF THE 16th President is so dramatic, so intriguing, so inspiring, as to catch one's heart, imagination, and hope. It begins simply and proceeds to build to its tragic climax, all the while steadied and guided by its wise, poetic, and visionary star, Abraham Lincoln. He was and is, quite simply, one of our great Americans. It is amazing and humbling to the people of Kansas to know that this story begins in Kansas, for Abraham Lincoln came here in December 1859 to give his first campaign speech — in essence, the same speech he would give two months later at the Cooper Institute, in New York City, and the one that critics claim propelled him toward the presidency.

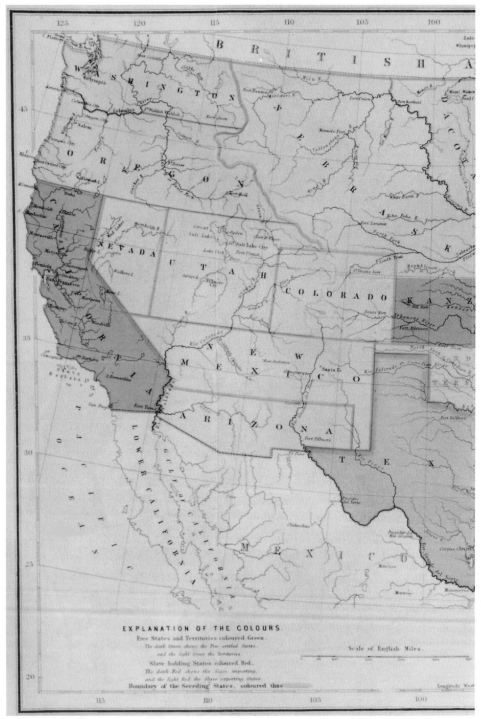

The original 1857 map of **Free and Slave-Holding States**, housed in the Library of Congress, indicates the following as **Free Territories**: Arizona, Colorado, "Dacotah," Indian Territory (Oklahoma), Nebraska, Nevada, New Mexico, Oregon, Utah, and Washington. **Free-Settled States** include California, Connecticut, Illinois, Indiana, Iowa, "Kanzas," Maine, Massachusetts, Michigan, Minnesota, New

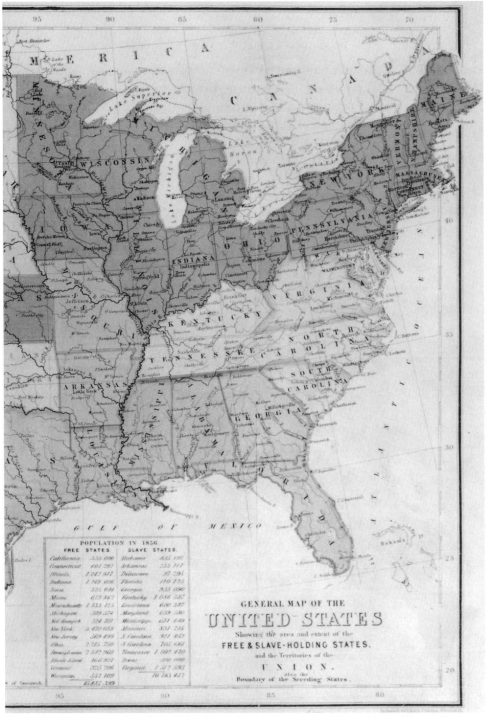

Hampshire, New Jersey, New York, Ohio, Pennsylvania, Rhode Island, Vermont, and Wisconsin. **Slave-Holding States — Importing** include Alabama, Arkansas, Florida, Georgia, Louisiana, Mississippi, Missouri, and Texas. **Slave-Holding States — Exporting** include Delaware, Kentucky, Maryland, North Carolina, South Carolina, Tennessee, and Virginia.

To understand the political environment in Kansas during Abraham Lincoln's visit, one would have to begin in 1820 with the Missouri Compromise. This act declared that all territories north of Missouri's southern border would be *free* and all territories south of its southern border would be *slave*. It was hoped that this would maintain some sort of balance in a Union trying to exist, half-slave and half-free. But this balance was upset by the Kansas-Nebraska Act proposed by Stephen A. Douglas in 1854, which allowed the people of a territory to determine the future of slavery in their state through a vote of popular sovereignty. The Kansas-Nebraska Act strongly impacted the territory of Kansas as proslavery and free-stater forces rushed their representative people into the territory to influence the outcome of territorial voting. These new residents, with their extremist

Senator Stephen A. Douglas.
*Kansas State Historical Society, Topeka*

views, conflicted in battles that would gain Kansas its nickname of "Bloody Kansas" and, essentially, begin the Civil War in Kansas years before the first shot was fired at Fort Sumter in Charleston Harbor, South Carolina, in April 1861. The mutual hatred and bitterness sparked a vicious cycle of attacks, reprisals, and counter-reprisals. As one Kansan later remarked, "The Devil came to the border, liked it, and decided to stay awhile."[1] The Border War, between Kansas and Missouri, was bloody, vicious, and complex, fought by people with many different purposes — some had moral convictions against slavery, some political aspirations, some wanted wealth or land, and others just wanted to rob and plunder. This guerrilla warfare would include such infamous and famous people as John Brown, James H. Lane, William Clarke Quantrill, and Charles Jennison.

John Brown had come to Kansas from New York state with visions of a slave-free nation burning in his soul. He took a strong moral position against slavery and there was a fervor in his belief that was not to be denied. Brown was over six-feet tall, grim-faced, and, when he was young, clean-shaven. At the end of his life, his long, white beard and hair belied his 59 years and most thought him to be much older. John Brown joined 5 sons — of his 20 children — who had moved to Kansas before him, and settled near Osawatomie where he soon became a guerrilla leader. Brown made many raids into Missouri to free slaves and, at one time, made a 1,000-mile trek to Canada to find a home for them. In a "divine mission" retaliation for the killing of five free-staters and the first sacking of Lawrence, he and four of his sons and three other men dragged five proslavery settlers from their cabins near Pottawatomie Creek and hacked them to death. This, for a time, stopped the harassment of free-staters in the area.

Eventually John Brown came to believe that fighting in Kansas was not going to accomplish his purpose of eradicating slavery, and he began to look to a much larger plan, a plan that included an attack on the federal

John Brown in the summer of 1859.
*Kansas State Historical Society, Topeka*

armory at Harpers Ferry, Virginia. Brown intended to use the guns and ammunition from the armory to arm the slaves and encourage them to rise up and fight for their own freedom. But the plan failed; Brown was captured by Colonel Robert E. Lee, tried, and hanged December 2, 1859, the second day of Lincoln's visit to Kansas. John Brown went to the scaffold willingly and fearlessly, for he knew that he was worth more to the cause martyred than spared, and he believed that heaven would be his reward. Such notables as writer and poet Ralph Waldo Emerson and abolitionist Wendell Phillips believed that Brown was a hero, and Northern troops and civilians sang the folk song "John Brown's Body Lies A-mouldering in the Grave, But His Soul Is Marching On."

Although Brown's tactics might remain controversial, he played a defining role in that he was able to rally many Northerners behind his cause and draw a clear line against slavery, outlining the issue for many people of the North and the South. One may not agree with John Brown's actions, but fervor or devotion are not questioned. Along with Harriet Beecher Stowe and her book, *Uncle Tom's Cabin*, John Brown served an important role as a catalyst in bringing the darkness of slavery to the forefront and forcing a nation to see it in the light.

James H. Lane, the first U.S. Senator from Kansas, was another key player in Bloody Kansas during those early territorial days. Although Lane was an accused unfaithful husband, a liar, and had killed a man, he may have done more than any other man to bring freedom to Kansas. Called the "King" in Kansas, Lane stood over six-feet tall, with hair standing out in every direction. There was a reckless intensity about his visage, sparked by his deep-set eyes. Senator John J. Ingalls described Lane:

> His energy was tireless and his activity indefatigable. No night was too dark, no storm too wild, no heat or cold too excessive, no distance too great, to delay his meteoric pilgrimages, with dilapidated garb and equipage, across the trackless prairies from convention to convention. His oratory was voluble and incessant, without logic, learning, rhetoric or grace; but the multitude to whom he perpetually appealed hung upon his hoarse and harsh harangues with the rapture of devotees upon

Senator James H. Lane.
*Kansas State Historical
Society, Topeka*

the oracular rhapsodies of a prophet and responded to his apostrophies with frenzied enthusiasm. He gained the prize which he sought with such fevered ambition.[2]

As author Noble Prentis says, "He talked like none of the rest."[3] Lane had a husky, rasping, blood-curdling whisper that he supported with a menacing bony forefinger, almost always accompanied by his famous exclamation of "*Great God.*" Ingalls described Lane's style of speaking:

> His voice is a series of transitions from the broken scream of a maniac to the hoarse, rasping gutterals of a Dutch butcher in the last gasp of inebriation; the construction of his sentences is loose and disjointed; his diction is a pudding of slang, profanity and solecism; and yet the electric shock of his extraordinary eloquence thrills like the blast of a trumpet; the magnetism of his manner, the fire of his glance, the studied earnestness of his utterances, finds a sudden response in the will of his audience, and he sways them like a field of reeds shaken by the wind.[4]

But Lane's charismatic personality assured him of many willing followers, whether fighting the proslavery supporters or making political speeches. Associate Judge Samuel Kingman, of Kansas, described Lane as

> . . . a man who can stand up before a crowd of five hundred men, two hundred and fifty of whom are ready to hang him to the next tree, and at the end of half an hour have them all cheering for him.[5]

Certainly the crowd was always there; an announcement that he was to speak "called the aged from the chimney-corner and the children from their play,"[6] as Lane was a great orator. Though never commissioned

John James Ingalls on November 11, 1862.
*Kansas State Historical Society, Topeka*

until Lincoln appointed him a Brigadier General of volunteers in 1861, Lane, early on in the conflict, gave himself the rank of Brigadier General and it was never taken from him. He and his "Jayhawkers" — sometimes called "Kansas Red Legs" for the red leggings they wore — aggressively fought the Border Ruffians from Missouri. Two famous "Red Legs" who at one time rode with Lane and would later become Union Army scouts were James Butler "Wild Bill" Hickok and William Frederick "Buffalo Bill" Cody.[7]

Lane, even though Lincoln initially forbade it, was the first to recruit blacks and Indians into his "Tri-color Brigade" during the Civil War.[8] Kansas had been fighting for so long by the time the Civil War began, that there were not enough men to cover all of the areas where soldiers were needed. Because Kansas was the destination for many free blacks and there were several Indian reservations in the state, blacks and Indians were a good source of recruits for Lane. John Speer, in his biography of Lane, reported a conversation with Lane concerning this issue.

> . . . I was walking down Pennsylvania avenue, in Washington, with Lane, he told me that he had just received authority to organize three regiments of white and two of colored soldiers in Kansas; and when I asked in amazement to see the order to enlist the colored troops, he informed me that it was a VERBAL promise from the President that he would see that they were clothed and subsisted until such time as they could be brought into line armed and equipped for battle; and on August 4, 1862, he opened a recruiting office in Leavenworth for both white and colored troops. He stumped the entire State, appealing to the patriotism of the people, in a campaign of unparalleled energy and power; and in less than six weeks he had the Eleventh, Twelfth and Thirteenth Kansas regiments organized, and a nucleus for the First and Second Colored infantry, the First Colored Battery thrown in for good count, and all completed before the ides of October. He appointed all the officers, under the authority of the President — no recognition being given to the Kansas State Government. I am not explaining. I am only attesting a fact. Abraham Lincoln did it.[9]

James Lane, a lawyer with considerable political experience in Indiana, came to Kansas and homesteaded a cabin near Lawrence, which was the home of the free-staters. After fighting a duel over a questionable relationship with another woman, he returned to Indiana following his wife, whom he was seeking to divorce. The Kansas Legislature failed to grant Lane's divorce, but granted one to his wife — the Lanes would later remarry. Lane admitted that he might be "quite a man with the ladies."[10]

When Lane returned to Lawrence, another homesteader confronted him — Gaius Jenkins, with whom Lane had quarreled over a claim and water rights. Gunfire was exchanged, and Jenkins lay dead. Lane was never charged with murder; some say it was because of his persuasive way with words.

Regardless of his tactics, antics, or opinions, Lane reigned supreme in Kansas in those early territorial and statehood days, and he played a key role in bringing Kansas into the Union as a free state. He was everywhere, leading his soldiers, addressing a convention, reporting on a platform; if there was an event, Lane was there. He was, in the phrase invented by Daniel Webster Wilder, "One of our things,"[11] in the same way one might refer to a Kansas tornado.

While campaigning in 1864, Lane promised the same office to 17 men. In fact, he had promised so many offices that in 1865 there was a near riot outside of his house in Washington, D.C. The police came to break up the crowd, and the incident, much to Lane's chagrin, was reported in the papers. In an attempt to handle part of the problem, he invited the 17 men to meet with him and spoke to them in the typical Lane style:

> Gentlemen, I was in a tight spot last winter when I promised each of you the marshalship for the district of Kansas. I am in a tighter spot today. What I did last winter, I did with the purest of motives. I wished re-election not simply for my own personal good, but for the good of the state of Kansas. I brought that state into the Union. I am having the Indians cleared out of it and put in the Indian Territory. I have promised all the public land in the state to railroads. In fact, I have promised so much land, the people may have to move out to make room for the railroads. In a few short years, Kansas will be gridironed with railroads, and there is every reason to believe that our state will be one of the greatest in the Union. All of this I have done. I

thought Kansas needed me in the senate, and for that reason I made promises which I cannot now fulfill. If I have deceived you, gentlemen, I believe that heaven will forgive me. But you, who should have voted for me from the purest and highest impulses, were impelled only by sordid motives. You sold your votes, and I do not think any of you worthy in the sight of heaven to hold an office. I renounce you all, and in the interest of the state of Kansas I will select an entirely new man. Good evening, gentlemen.[12]

Abraham Lincoln was not immune to Lane's abilities to persuade, which was due mainly to an event in Washington, D.C., soon after Lincoln was elected President. In April 1861, shortly after Lane and Samuel Pomeroy were chosen to be the first United States Senators from Kansas,

Fort Sumter, South Carolina, was fired upon, and the Civil War had begun. Washington, D.C., was in an unsettled state with sympathetic Southerners either leaving or breathing threats of attacks. The loyalty of the neighboring states of Maryland and Virginia was questioned, and rumors that President Lincoln was in danger of assassination were spread around the Capital.

Pomeroy described later in his reminiscences that he and Lane, after arriving in Washington, had made speeches in front of the Willard Hotel where they were staying. Pomeroy

Senator Samuel Pomeroy.
*Kansas State Historical Society, Topeka*

said he spoke first and then Lane climbed up on a dry-goods box to make his speech.

> . . . The first night of our stay at Willard's in Washington, we were called upon for speeches, in the midst of that excited crowd which filled Pennsylvania Avenue on the night of April 13th, 1861, when Sumter surrendered.
>
> . . . When Lane took the stand, just as I had left it, there was a tremendendous shout from the rebel crowd — "Mob him!" "Mob him!" "Hang him!" etc., etc.
>
> Lane was naturally passionate and excitable. I saw at the moment he was terribly aroused. His eyes flashed more fire than came from the street lamps; and his tremendous voice was elevated to the highest pitch. He repeated in his first words the noise of the crowd, crying out, "Mob; and be damned! Mob; and be damned! I have a hundred men from Kansas in this crowd, all armed; all fighting men; just from the victorious fields of Kansas! They will shoot every damned man of you who again cries, 'Mob,' 'Mob.'"
>
> Now the other side cheered Lane with all their might; and then repeated it again and again. The click of cocking pistols was heard all through that crowd, as men put their hands upon revolvers. Order was restored. In a moment more it was as still as the chamber of death. No man seemed to know who stood next to him.
>
> General Lane then went on uninterruptedly, and finished one of the most impassioned and eloquent speeches he ever made. His denunciation of the firing upon the flag at Sumter, of secession, and of slavery was most terrific; and his appeals for freedom — consitutional freedom; for "Liberty under Law," might, as it then seemed to me, have been heard across the Potomac, if not at Arlington! For his voice reverberated among the hills, where Lee had gone home to sleep.[13]

There was fear for Lincoln's safety. Lane, newly arrived, was eager to be a part of the solution. Earlier, when Lincoln was ready to proceed to the nation's Capital for his inauguration, Lane had offered a bodyguard of Kansas men and Lincoln had declined the offer, believing in the loyalty of the American people.[14] However, the threatened assassination of Lincoln at Baltimore, Maryland, proved Lane right. Now everyone seemed to agree there was a need for such protection. Word was sent out to call all Kansans to Lane's room at the Willard Hotel. When the group had gathered, Lane was presented a ceremonial sword by Major David Hunter. Corpulent Samuel Pomeroy reported in later memoirs an embarrassing incident that occurred that night.

> I now remember that though Senator elect, I, took the oath, and put on the uniform of a private soldier, and stood in my place in the ranks.
> There was one incident which amused the men with me more than it did myself. It was this: in trying to buckle the belt of a United States uniform about me, none could be found long enough. So to the amusement of others, I had to cut a hole in one end of the strap, and splice it with a string. With my belt thus fastened, I did duty until honorably mustered out.[15]

The Frontier Guard, made up of 120 men from Kansas, was organized on April 14th. On the night of April 18th, General James Lane as Captain, along with Colonel Mark Delahay as First Lieutenant, Captain J. B. Stockton as Second Lieutenant, and, as Privates, Dan Anthony, Thomas Ewing, Jr., Samuel Pomeroy, A. C. Wilder, M. J. Parrott, and many other Kansans were furnished with arms and ammunition and marched to the White House[16] where they bivouacked in the East Room. Authors John G. Nicolay and John Hay described the colorful scene:

> . . . after spending the evening in an exceedingly rudimentary squad drill, under the light of the gorgeous gas chandeliers, they disposed themselves in picturesque bivouac on the brilliant-patterned velvet carpet — perhaps the most luxurious cantonment which American soldiers have ever enjoyed. Their motley composition, their anomalous surroundings, the extraordinary emergency, their mingled awkwardness and earnestness, rendered the scene a medley of bizarre contradictions, — a blending of masquerade and tragedy, of grim humor and realistic seriousness, — a combination of Don Quixote and Daniel Boone altogether impossible to describe.[17]

Another account of a personal observer:

> This well-known resort is one of the most beautiful and mag-
> nificent halls in the country. Such a post of honor, on such an
> emergent occasion — for the President had heard the rumor that
> day that himself and Gen. Scott were in danger of assassination
> from a Virginia party that night — was no ordinary compli-
> ment. Other companies, of no little notoriety and experi-
> ence, were in the city, but this distinction was reserved for
> Kansas.
>
> That night, Kansas had supreme possession of the White
> House, and fifty of her "Old Guard" slept sweetly on the Pres-
> ident's rich Brussels, with their arms stacked in martial line
> down the center of the hall, while two long rows of Kansas
> ex-Governors, Senators, Judges, Editors, Generals and Jay-
> hawkers were dozing upon each side, and the sentinels made
> regular beats around them. . . .[18]

These Kansans were clearly battle tested, having fought for freedom
in their state for many years. They were serious about their assignment. According to the *Washington Evening Star* account on April 19,
1861,

> Beside the regular guard which has been stationed in the
> vicinity of the President's house for some time, a guard of
> sixty under the command of Gen. James H. Lane, of Kansas,
> occupied the east room and slept upon their arms last night.
> This company has been organized but a day or two, yet a
> large force is already enrolled, and the corps increasing rapidly.
> Late in the evening the President attempted to enter the east
> room, but as the sentinel at the door had received orders to
> admit no one without the countersign, Mr. Lincoln was
> forced to beat a retreat, to the no small amusement of the
> company.

Back in Kansas there was much pride that their sons were given such a
lofty responsibility, and James Lane was heralded as a hero. An article
from the April 18, 1861, *Leavenworth Conservative* noted:

It will be seen by our telegraphic report that Gen. James H. Lane has been called upon by the War Department to take charge of one thousand Union Guards in Washington. It does not surprise us that the Defender of Freedom in Kansas is honored with a high position the moment he arrives at the seat of Government, and we are now willing to bet our last cent (dollars are played out in Kansas) that Washington will not be taken. When old Jim gives the word, "Up, boys, and at them," there will be an awful scattering among the rebels.[19]

The Frontier Guard was disbanded on May 3, 1861, when troops from the North took over the guarding of the Capital. On April 27th, they marched to the White House for the last time and received President Lincoln's thanks for their service.

The Frontier Guard, under the command of Gen. Lane, of Kansas, who have for the last week been stationed in and around the White House, by invitation of President Lincoln, waited upon him yesterday afternoon [*April 26th*] at the Executive Mansion.

The company formed at Gen. Lane's headquarters at Willard's hotel, to the number of one hundred and twenty, and marched, under the direction of their leader, to the President's.

The Guard was ushered into the East Room and formed around it in double file.

Upon the President's entrance, the Guard was introduced to him by Gen. Lane, who also introduced Col. Vaughan, of Kansas, as the orator for the occasion, who addressed him in substance as follows:

"Mr. President: Permit me to introduce to you the Frontier Guard, a company formed under the leadership of Gen. James H. Lane, for the protection of the capital of the nation, at a time when great danger threatened the liberties of this our common country.

"A large proportion of them have been in situations of trial; when the dark cloud of peril overshadowed our Western borders, under the command of their gallant leader they rallied around the stars and stripes, and drove the invader from their soil.

"And now, once again, in this our darkest hour, they respond to our country's call, and offer their lives and all they have to support the Constitution and vindicate the majesty of the law.

"You and I, Mr. President, (pardon me for using my name in connection with yours,) you and I are Southern born, and although deprecating the shedding of fraternal blood, yet if this Government under your administration is preserved, there are thousands of our brethren at the South, Union-loving and true men, who if they can be protected, will flock to the flag of the nation, and rally around the glorious stars and stripes, and aid us in preserving them intact and pure, and handing them down unsullied to our posterity. And I doubt not, sir, there are many even in my own native state of South Carolina, that yet love this Union, and who dare not speak, for treason and disunion are abroad in the land, and their hands are tied.

"It is the response of every man here, and I am instructed by them to say, so far as they are concerned, *No compromise with rebels.*

"And now, sir, the Frontier Guard holds itself subject to orders. Should their services be needed in any capacity, to assist in the enforcement of the laws of the country, to preserve inviolate the Constitution of the United States, they are ready. Brave and true men are here, who have been proved in times of trial and danger and found to be equal to the task and ready for any emergency. Although some of us propose to leave the city if our services are no longer required for its security, yet, if necessary, every man will be at his post to protect it.

"Permit me once more to introduce the Frontier Guard."

The President replied briefly, thanking the Guard for services performed, and for the patriotic feeling which prompted their efforts. After the very pleasant interview, the Guard marched back to Willard's and exchanged compliments with each other, and adjourned till the next meeting.[20]

Samuel Pomeroy also shared in his reminiscences the capturing of the first rebel flag by the Frontier Guard. The event is shared in the words of Captain J. B. Stockton who led the detachment.

> I captured the first rebel flag of the rebellion, Apr. 18th, 1861, at or near Falls Church, Virginia. Gen'l Scott had given me orders to take a detachment of Frontier Guards and ascertain the strength of the rebels at that place. This order I obeyed. Upon our approach toward a company we saw drilling upon parade, we charged. They left the place rapidly, not having time to take down their flag, which was fastened to the top of a flagstaff without halyards. Returning I delivered that flag to Gen'l. Lane at our headquarters. The next morning it was seen hanging out of the window of Lane's room at Willard's Hotel, across which Lane had written, in large letters. *"Captured by the Frontier Guards upon the sacred soil of Virginia!"* In an hour or two more than ten thousand people stood looking at the flag.
> Mr. Lincoln soon sent for me to bring the flag to the White House. About one o'clock Lane and I went up. The Cabinet was in session, and Gen'l Scott called also.
> Upon our handing it to Mr. Lincoln, who sat at the end of a long table, raising it up, with flag in hand he walked over to Gen'l Scott, "what a miserable rag that is to fight for!" "Yes," replied the General, "but it convinces me that Gen'l Lee has not yet reached Richmond. He will have a better looking flag."[21]

From that time on, the grateful Lincoln was also in the grasp of Lane's magnetism and it was known in Kansas that if you wanted anything from the President, have James Lane ask for it. However, Lane must have been somewhat of a pest to the President, who is reported to have given this comment to Governor Thomas Carney of Kansas in 1864, which might explain Lane's ability to get so much from Lincoln.

> He (Lane) knocks at my door every morning. You know he is a very persistent fellow and hard to put off. I don't see you very often, and have to pay attention to him.[22]

Lane continued to support Lincoln throughout his presidency, with one exception. During the Republican Convention of June 1864, in Baltimore, there was a move afoot to nominate someone other than Lincoln. Republicans were concerned that the slowly on-going war and Lincoln's failure to end it were going to ensure the election of a Democrat in the fall. According to William O. Stoddard, one of Lincoln's secretaries who was himself a member, the Union League had been formed in the summer of 1862 at the silent urging of President Lincoln to help combat the many secret organizations and lodges that were furthering the Southern position for the upcoming election. Twelve men became the League's executive group, called the Grand Council.

The Union League had organized local councils in most cities and towns of the North. The Grand Council, that included leading men from all parts of the country, had met in Washington in the summer of 1863. Many spoke against Lincoln and his administration — one of them being Senator James Lane. Governor Thomas Carney of Kansas joined Lane in his condemnation of Lincoln. Stoddard in his position of corresponding secretary was on the platform and angrily responded to what he considered to be unjust claims. After his remarks, the meeting was adjourned, to be reconvened at the Republican Convention the following year. Stoddard continues:

> The first man to grab my hand and thank me for convincing him against his will was Senator Jim Lane of Kansas, who declared loudly, "Henceforth I am an unquestioning supporter of Abraham Lincoln. I was misled."[23]

The Grand Council of the Union League met the night before the Republican Convention to select its candidate. This preliminary convention, though unofficial, would nevertheless settle everything. The men of the Grand Council were the delegates of power that would gather in the "Wigwam" for the National Convention the following day. In order to preserve an appearance of unanimity, the debating would be concluded at the Grand Council, and its actions would be confirmed at the National Convention. The move against Lincoln was much as it had been the previous year. Lincoln was characterized as incompetent and unfit, with many calling for a more capable President. When Lane perceived that the inflamed rhetoric was opposing Lincoln, he rose and walked down the middle aisle and began to speak passionately:

> Mr. President, Gentlemen of the Grand Council: For a man to produce pain in another man by pressing upon a wounded spot requires no great degree of strength, and he who presses is not entitled to any emotion of triumph at the agony expressed by the sufferer. Neither skill nor wisdom has been exercised in the barbaric process. For a man, an orator, to produce an effect upon sore and weary hearts, gangrened with bitter disappointments, so stirring them up, even to passion and to folly, demands no high degree of oratorical ability. It is an easy thing to do, as we have seen this evening. Almost anybody could do it.
>
> For a man to take such a crowd as this now is, so sore and sick at heart, and now so stung and aroused to passionate folly, now so infused with a delusive hope for the future, as well as address himself to such an assembly, and turn the tide of its passion and excitement in the opposite direction — that were a task worthy of the highest, greatest effort of human oratory. I am no orator at all; but to precisely that task I now set myself, with absolute certainty of success. All that is needful is that the truth should be set forth plainly, now that the false has done its worst.
>
> I am speaking individually to each man here. Do you, sir, know in this broad land, and can you name to me, one man whom you could or would trust, before God, that he would have done better in this matter than Abraham Lincoln has done, and to whom you would be now more willing to trust the unforeseen emergency or peril which is to come? That unforeseen peril, that perplexing emergency, that step in the dark, is right before us, and we are here to decide by whom it should be made for the Nation. Name your other man.
>
> We shall come together to be watched, in breathless listening, by all this country — by all the civilized world, — and if we shall seem to waver as to our set purpose, we destroy hope; and if we permit private feeling, as to-night, to break forth into discussion, we discuss defeat; and if we nominate any other man than Abraham Lincoln, we nominate ruin. Gentlemen of the Grand Council of the Union League, I have done.[24]

Lane spoke convincingly. The Council resolved to endorse Lincoln, and the next day, at the Republican Party's formal convention, Lane nominated him. During the same convention, Lane was credited with choosing Andrew Johnson for Vice President and convincing the convention to allow the delegates from reconstructed Arkansas, Louisiana, and Tennessee to vote.[25]

According to John Speer, James Lane's biographer, Lincoln chose Lane to open the campaign of 1864 with a speech at the Cooper Institute in New York City. Speaking before the Union League Campaign Club, Lane reviewed Lincoln's administration and managed to restrain himself from the public utterances that usually characterized his public addresses.[26]

Lane campaigned tirelessly for Lincoln, devoting his time largely to Kansas and Missouri. Spurred on by Lincoln's re-appointment of General Samuel Curtis to military command in Kansas, which Kansans approved, and by Lane's lead, the Kansas Legislature, with only one dissenting vote, adopted a resolution endorsing Lincoln's re-election.[27] Lincoln carried Kansas by a margin of 17,000 to 4,000. Lane's important leadership for Lincoln must have certainly been a factor in his reappointment as U.S. Senator by the Kansas Legislature in January 1865.

James Lane, whose own behavior was not always "civilized," wanted his daughter, Annie, to be a refined lady, so he chose to put her in the Sisters of Charity Academy for young girls in Leavenworth. When Lane and Chester Norris, free-staters, both of whom had daughters at the Academy, would visit the Sisters, Mother Vincent, who was then the Mother Superior, would expound upon her Southern views. Sister Mary Buckner, in her book *History of the Sisters of Charity of Leavenworth, Kansas*, recalled:

> She said once to them, "You are the real Secessionists." They assured her she was mistaken, that they were true Unionists. "No," she persisted, "all Protestants are Secessionists, and they should be whipped back into the Union — that is, into the True Church."[28]

Mother Vincent, who was intensely Southern in sentiment, expressed her opinions freely whenever she met any of the abolitionists. Not all of the Sisters shared her views, as Sister Buckner remembered.

> Mother Xavier was just as much in favor of the North as Mother Vincent was of the South, but she was so prudent in her remarks that no one not most intimately acquainted with her would have known that she had a strong predilection for "the boys in blue."[29]

According to the Sisters of Charity records, Annie Lane was at the academy in Leavenworth during the sacking of Lawrence in 1863 when the Lanes' home was burned.

James Lane's last visit to Leavenworth was at the time of his death. He returned to Fort Leavenworth in July 1866, to visit his brother-in-law, Captain McCall. Lane was not well and was feeling despondent. According to John Speer, there were possibly three reasons for this despondency.[30] Speer believed that the primary cause was insanity. Supposedly, Lane had premonitions of his own insanity and suggested that he be taken to an insane asylum after he attempted to jump from a hotel window in St. Louis. Others reported that Lane was suffering from softening of the brain. There is a possibility that Lane might have been suffering from dementia, a part of the third stage of syphilis.

The second cause for Lane's despondency was his vote to uphold President Andrew Johnson's veto of the Civil Rights Act. Although Lane claimed the purpose in his vote was to reconcile the President and the Republican Congress, he was condemned and snubbed by his constituents who were adamantly opposed to the veto. Lane had been accustomed to patronage from President Lincoln, and after Lincoln's death, Lane was anxious to continue his influence with President Johnson. This desire might have been behind Lane's pledge of support of the veto.

Regardless of Lane's reasons, the result was politically disastrous. In addition to his congressional colleagues, Lane incurred the anger of the people of Kansas. He received a telegram from them warning that a vote for Johnson could be his political ruin. When Kansans learned of Lane's vote, he was denounced across the state. On February 3, 1891, the *Lawrence Daily Record* charged:

> Lane is nothing, if not radical, and when he ceases to act with

the radicals, he will play out and disappear from the political stage forever.

A third cause of Lane's lack of well-being was the accusation, in an article in the *Chicago Tribune*, of his accepting of bribes in awarding Indian contracts. Lane denied the charge and traced the article to its supposed source, Colonel George Deitzler of Lawrence, Kansas. Deitzler, when confronted, issued a statement that he had no knowledge of such a bribe. These last two events caused Lane's popularity to plummet.

Some claimed that another issue influenced Lane's death — the hanging of Mrs. Mary Surratt for her involvement in the assassination of Lincoln. After the trial of the John Wilkes Booth conspirators, the military commission sentenced four to death, including Surratt. However, a majority of the commission signed a petition requesting that President Andrew Johnson commute Surratt's sentence to life imprisonment. Judge Advocate General Joseph Holt, who brought the results to the White House for the President's review, was a close friend of Lincoln. Hoping for the execution of Surratt, Holt arranged the trial documents so that the President would be unlikely to see the petition. Johnson, who was ill at the time, approved the sentence and gave orders that he not be disturbed by anyone requesting mercy for the prisoners. Consequently, Lane and Preston King, a personal adviser and close friend of President Johnson, denied Anna Surratt entrance when she came to plead for the life of her mother. As a result, Surratt was hanged along with Lewis Payne, David E. Herold, and George A. Atzerodt. King and Lane would eventually both take their own lives and some asserted it was remorse over the Surratt affair.[31]

One can imagine that all of these circumstances took their toll on Lane and led to his depressed state that day at Fort Leavenworth. He expressed a desire to take a ride, and was accompanied in a carriage by Captain McCall and Captain Frank Adams. When they stopped to open a gate, Lane jumped out and exclaimed, "Goodbye, gentlemen," and discharged a revolver into his mouth. The ball passed upward through his brain.

Lane died ten days later, in Leavenworth, on July 11, 1866, a little more than a year after Lincoln was assassinated. "The King was dead."[32] Yet, for all of his peculiarities, Senator James Lane was relentless in his determined pursuit of freedom for Kansas and deserves recognition for the tremendous impact he made upon the future of Kansas and ultimately the United States.

William Clarke Quantrill was James Lane's nemesis and the commander of Missouri guerrillas, known as "Pukes," "Border Ruffians," or "Bushwhackers" by their Kansas enemies. Unlike John Brown whose beliefs were based on a moral, religious conviction, or James Lane who desired political power, William Quantrill was an outlaw who desired to fill his pockets with the booty acquired from robbing and looting raids. Personal vengeance was also an issue. Even though some historians do not agree with the accuracy, two men who rode with Quantrill — Harrison Trow and John McCorkle — tell the same story of how he went "bad." Quantrill and Lane's paths crossed for the first time in 1857, when, according to Quantrill, he and his brother, who were on their way to California, were attacked by James Lane's Red Legs at the Little Cottonwood River in Kansas. Quantrill was seriously wounded and his brother was killed. The Red Legs took all of their victims' belongings and their slave, and left Quantrill to die of his injuries. After three days, he was found by a Shawnee Indian who nursed him back to health. Determined to avenge the death of his brother, Quantrill, using the alias of Charles Hart, went to Lawrence and joined James Lane and the company that was responsible for his brother's death. The company lost more men that year than any other, many in mysterious ways. Anytime Quantrill would ride out alone with another Jayhawker, that man would mysteriously die with a bullet wound in the middle of his forehead. After a year, Quantrill had covertly killed all of the men involved in his brother's death, except two. In his final act as a free-stater, he conspired, with his comrades, to raid one of the richer border plantations in Missouri, belonging to Morgan Walker, and steal its slaves. Little did the Jayhawkers know that Quantrill had arranged an ambush with Morgan Walker. He led them to the plantation and boldly knocked on the door. The door suddenly opened and Quantrill lept into the house leaving his fellow Kansans to be greeted with shotgun blasts from the slave owner and his men. Six Jayhawkers were killed on the spot and the two who escaped were tracked down and killed by the traitor Quantrill and his proslavery companions.[33]

Thus were the last killers disposed of, and Quantrill dropped his alias and became a committed Bushwhacker. A few days later, Quantrill wrote to Lane telling him everything that had transpired and the fate of the many lost men from Lane's Jayhawker company. He also said that he was going to Virginia to get a commission from Jefferson Davis and, in essence, challenged Lane to war on the border. Lane, never one to pass up a challenge, sent his Jayhawkers into Missouri, beginning the long battle not just between Kansas and Missouri, or proslavery and free-stater, but a much more personal one between himself and Quantrill. The battle would ultimately culminate in the burning of Lawrence, which was in part an excuse for Quantrill to kill Lane and burn his town.

William Quantrill wore the Bushwhacker uniform of a hunting shirt and pants. His small head perched atop a long neck was balanced by his brimmed, black hat and his handle-bar mustache. Amazingly, without his hat, his softly curled hair and smooth cheeks gave him an almost gentle countenance. But Quantrill and his men were far from gentle. His band was made up of "tough young Missourians with Southern sympathies who resented jayhawker raids, and of border ruffians and outlaws. . . ."[34] Some of the more infamous guerrillas to ride with Quantrill were "Bloody Bill" Anderson, who bedecked the bridle of his horse with human scalps, the sadistic George Todd, Cole and James Younger, and Frank and Jesse James.[35]

William Clarke Quantrill, the leader of the Missouri guerrillas.

Many of these men continued their lawless ways after the war was over.

Once he was permanently committed to the Border Ruffians, Quantrill planned and carried out many raids into Kansas, killing, plundering, and destroying property. In 1862 alone, he sacked the village of Aubrey, shot down helpless civilians "like so many hogs" at Olathe, and reduced the entire town of Shawnee to ashes.[36] His most well-known raid was at Lawrence, Kansas, on August 21, 1863, when he and about 450 men retaliated upon Lane and his hometown for the burning of Osceola, Missouri. Early on the morning of August 21st, the sleeping town was awakened by the sound of galloping horses, gunshots, and blood-curdling yells as Quantrill's Raiders descended upon Lawrence's citizens. All men who could be found — 150 — were killed and 100 homes and businesses were burned and another 100 damaged by fire.[37] Quantrill's goal of killing Lane as part of the raid was not realized, as Lane was able to escape into a cornfield and make his getaway.

The following events of the

Frank James.
*Kansas State Historical Society, Topeka*

Jesse Woodson James.
*Kansas State Historical Society, Topeka*

Quantrill's attack on Lawrence is depicted in this early print.

*Kansas State Historical Society, Topeka*

raid were related by Reverend H. D. Fisher, James Lane's chaplain, who survived:

> I was always an anti-slavery man of the most "anti" kind, and after I moved to Kansas, without any prominence having been given to my sentiments by myself, I found myself the object of the most vindictive hatred of the pro-slavery party of the region where I resided. My life was unsuccessfully sought several times. When the war broke out I went as a Chaplain. Most of the male members of my church went to the war, and I went as one of Jim Lane's chaplains.
>
> The news of my connection with the army, and of my being put in charge of contrabands, who were sent to Kansas, got abroad, and the rebels hated me worse than ever. They got my photograph and distributed it throughout the country, and it was fixed among them that I was to be shot whenever met. Once when I was sent up the river with a body of contrabands, not

being well, I went home for a little rest. I was living at Lawrence. The town had a few guns in the armory, and there was an understanding with the farmers of the surrounding country that upon the ringing of an alarm, they should come in and defend the town, but the coming of Quantrell and his men was a complete surprise. When the alarm was rung the arsenal was already captured and on fire. I was in bed, and heard, about 3 o'clock in the morning, horses galloping very rapidly away, and woke my wife, telling her that it was singular that horses should be galloping so fast so early in the morning; but she said she guessed it was some farmers who had been to a railroad meeting the evening before, and were hurrying back to their work. We lay and talked for some time. The children were going out that morning to get some grapes, and my wife thought she would call them earlier than usual, and herein, brethren, I see the hand of Providence. It was not yet daylight, but day was dawning. Having called the children, she went and looked out of the front door, and instantly called me: "Pa, the Rebels are in town." I said that could not be; but nevertheless, I sprang from the bed and ran to the door.

There they were just across the green, and just then they shot the United Brethren preacher, as he was milking his cow in his barn-yard. I rushed back into the house; my wife caught up her babe; I have four boys; one was on my wife's breast, another was by her side, and the two oldest were twelve and fourteen years old. We all rushed up the lot in which our house stood. Then I left my wife, and with the two oldest boys ran up the hill, but something seemed to tell me that I was running away from safety. So I told the boys to run on, and I would go back to mother. It was then in the gray light of morning, and the Rebels had divided into little squads and were ransacking the town, killing every man they found, and burning houses. My boys separated, the oldest getting with a neighbor's boy, Robert Winton, and while the two were running for life the soldiers saw them and fired a volley, killing poor Bobby and frightening my boy almost to death. He ran in and hid among some graves in the grave-yard. My younger son ran off on the prairie.

In fixing my cellar I had thrown up a bank of earth near the entrance, and I crept down there and laid myself between the mound of earth and the wall in such a way that the earth would partially screen me. I lay up close to the kitchen floor. I had not been there long, when four of Quantrell's men rode up to the house and demanded admittance. My wife went to the front door and let them in. They demanded whether I was not in the house or in the cellar. She replied: "My husband and two oldest boys ran off as soon as the firing began." The leader swore that he knew I was in the cellar. My wife replied that she had two young children by her, and that she did not want any more oaths uttered before them. "You have doubted my word," she replied, "you can look for yourselves." I lay so near the floor that I could hear every word that was said. The men called for a candle.

My wife replied that we did not burn candles. Then they wanted a lantern, but she said we hadn't any. They asked then, with an oath, what we did for a light. She replied that we burned kerosene in a lamp. Then they called for a lamp, and my wife had to get it, but the men in their eagerness to light it, turned the wick down in the oil. Failing to light it themselves, they called on my wife to light it.

"Why, you've ruined the lamp," said she; "it can't be lighted with the wick down in the oil."

"Haven't you another lamp." say they.

"Yes, there's one up stairs," said she, and they then ordered her to go and get it.

"Gentlemen," said she, "I can't do it. Your rudeness has so frightened me that I can scarcely hold my babe."

One of the men then offered to hold it for her, and took it from her arms. My poor wife then went and got the lamp, which they lighted and started on their search. They all cocked their revolvers and passed the word to kill me at sight, and started for the cellar. I laid myself as flat as I could, and turned my face toward the wall, for I knew my face was thinnest from ear to ear. The light came to the door.

I tell you, brethren, I just quit living. You have heard it said that when man is drowning all his past life comes up before him.

. . . I stood then before the judgment seat. I was a dead man. My heart ceased to beat. I already stood before my Judge. Brethren, what could I do, but just trust myself to the Lord.

The man who carried the light was tall, and providentially stooped so low in entering the cellar that the light shining against the bank of earth threw a shadow over me. They searched the cellar, but did not find me, and went back up stairs. My wife afterwards told me that when the men went down in the cellar, she took her babe and went into the parlor, and stood there holding her hand against one ear, and her babe against the other, expecting every moment to hear the report of the revolvers in the cellar, announcing the death of her husband.

The soldiers set fire to the house in several places, and leaving one of their number to prevent my wife from putting it out, departed. The man seemed to be touched with pity, and told her that if she wanted to save some furniture he would help her. My wife thinks that holding the babe in his arms touched his heart. She pleaded with him if he had any consideration for her helpless children to leave the house and let her put out the fire. He consented and left.

My wife then came to me and asked me whether it was all right between me and God. I am afraid they will come back and kill you yet, and it will be the greatest comfort to know that you felt prepared to die.

I told her that I felt that I was prepared to die.

Telling me to pray, she left me. It was not long before another party of Quantrell's men came, and in drunken tones — for the marauders had become intoxicated by this time — demanded whether I was in the house.

"Do you suppose," said my wife, confidently, "that he would stay here and you shooting and burning all over town? No; he left this morning as soon as the firing commenced, and unless some of you have shot him and killed him outside, he is safe. Some of your men were here this morning and searched the house. However, you may look for yourselves."

In this way she bluffed them. They set fire to the house, and left one, who drew his revolver on my wife, and said he would kill her if she tried to put it out. He stayed till the house was so far consumed that there was no possibility of saving it. My wife pulled up a carpet, and taking it to the yard, dropped it accidentally by the door.

My wife was afraid, and so was I, that I would be burned alive, for I had now no thought of doing anything but what my wife told me. The floor was on fire almost over me, and the flames were creeping nearer. My wife stood and threw water, pail after pail, on the floor, and was doing this when a neighbor, a Catholic woman, came and said: "Why, Mrs. Fisher, what are you doing? What good will it be to save the floor? Besides, you can't save it."

"I don't care what good it will do," replied my wife, "I am going to keep on wetting that floor."

But, finally, when she saw she could not save it, she asked the neighbor whether she could keep a secret. She then swore her by the Virgin Mary never to reveal it.

"Well, then," said my wife, "my husband is under that floor."

The soldiers were still everywhere, shooting and burning, and the air was filled with the shrieks of wounded and dying men, the wailings of widows and orphans, and the sound of falling buildings. My wife then called me to come out, and threw a dress over my shoulders. The two women picked up the carpet, and I crawled under it between them and so we proceeded to a small bush about four feet high, out in the yard.

There my wife saw four soldiers ready to fire. They were not a hundred yards off. Then, for the first time, the poor woman despaired. A pang then shot to her heart, and she gave up all for lost. Nevertheless, I slunk under the bush, and they threw the carpet over me.

"Save the chairs!" cried my wife; and they rushed to where the chairs were piled close to the burning building, and ran with them and flung them carelessly upon me, and piled up all that was saved of our household goods about me. The soldiers, evidently, thought the pile only a lot of household furniture, and left it unmolested.

I staid there till two hours after they left, and then gathered my wife and my four children — for the two boys had come back — and in the garden we knelt and thanked God for deliverance. Brethren, you don't know what it is to be thank-ful.[38]

While the raid on Lawrence would remain the outstanding Bush-whacker victory of the war, Quantrill looked toward an even larger accom-plishment — the assassination of President Abraham Lincoln. Quantrill and 30 followers, dressed in blue Federal uniforms and with forged identification papers, rode east in early 1865. Their Federal disguise worked well, but their mission was thwarted by John Wilkes Booth in Ford's Theater on April 14, 1865. According to author William Connelley, Quantrill was at the house of Jonathan Davis, judge of Spencer County, Kentucky, when he heard the news of Lincoln's assassination.

> President Lincoln had been assassinated the night before, Quantrill and all his band were drunk. He apologized to the ladies, saying: "Excuse us, ladies. We are a little in our cups today. The grand-daddy of all greenback, Abraham Lincoln, was shot in a theatre at Washington last night," Calling for glasses, they all drank, the cut-throat, "One-armed" Berry, pro-nouncing the following toast: "Here's to the death of Abraham Lincoln, hoping that his bones may serve in hell as a gridiron to dry Yankees on."[39]

Ironically, rather than the mission ending with Lincoln's death as Quantrill had hoped, it would end with his own death. He was fatally wounded in a fight with the Union Army in Spencer County, Kentucky, and died June 7, 1865.

Another colorful personality of the period was Charles R. Jennison, who commanded the famous Jayhawker Kansas Seventh. The term "Jayhawker" had actually become infamous for Missourians under Jen-nison's friend and forerunner James Montgomery. Montgomery and Jennison lived in Linn County, Kansas, and were known for their sudden and unexpected incursions into Missouri, to rob, plunder, and steal slaves.

These raids were likened to the swoop of a hawk pouncing on an unsuspecting and less capably larcenous bluejay; thus were the Kansans labeled Jayhawkers by Missourians.

Charles Jennison, like John Brown, was that confusing combination of outlaw and apostle. He had an ardent, almost religious, hatred of slavery but was not morally restrained from robbing and killing. His friends held him in the highest respect, describing him ". . . as a paragon of virtue, abounding in kindness, loyalty, generosity, gallantry, amiability, and a rollicking good humor. . . ."[40] They considered him a resourceful and worthy military leader. His enemies, on the other hand, called him ". . . a brigand leader, an outlaw, a coward and a murderer, a liar, blackleg and robber, a moral vagabond, a wily freebooter, a moral leper, a thieving wretch, the greatest thief of modern times and an infamous criminal."[41]

In 1858, at age 24, Jennison settled in Mound City, Kansas. He was a small man with a boyish face that belied his penchant for gambling and drinking. In spite of the fact that Jennison was semi-literate and wrote very poorly, he studied and took up the practice of medicine. Upon arriving in Mound City, he established a flourishing medical practice and became known as "Doc" Jennison. This vocation did not, however, satisfy his need to lead. Like Lane, he was very energetic and attracted followers by his enthusiastic high spirits, his daring attitude, and his flair for the dramatic. He soon had a group of 400 men ready to follow him on his Missouri raids. His name became such a terror in Vernon and Bates Counties in Missouri, he boasted, ". . . that Missouri mothers hushed their children to sleep with his name."[42]

The border of southern Missouri became a desolate wasteland due to the constant robbing and burning by Montgomery and Jennison. Jennison's techniques were so questionable and there was such an outcry against him that the Territorial Governor Samuel Medary offered a reward of $1,000 for his arrest. Federal troops searched unsuccessfully for him, and he was ultimately saved by the outbreak of the Civil War. By then considered very qualified to be a military leader, Jennison was commissioned as a Colonel to lead the Seventh of Kansas. Even though criticized, he allowed the Kansas Seventh to continue the murderous forays and plundering proclivities into Missouri. When he learned that the Seventh was being sent to New Mexico, he resigned in April 1862. He, unfortunately, also encouraged many of his men to leave the Seventh, which they did. He was arrested for this action but eventually released.

Charles Jennison in 1861.                          *Kansas State Historical Society, Topeka*

Jennison returned to Kansas and, some believe, became involved again with the Red Legs. This group was possibly formed by deserters from the old Kansas Seventh, who returned to their robbing and pillaging ways. During this time he was appointed by Senator Lane to raise a regiment of ex-slaves who had escaped to Kansas.

Subsequent to the Lawrence massacre, Jennison was recommissioned and charged with raising a regiment of cavalry to be known as the Fifteenth of Kansas. In his recruiting speeches, he promised to vindicate the murdered men of Lawrence by leading them into Missouri "to shoot, kill, burn and confiscate until Lawrence and her murdered citizens were avenged."[43] These speeches were very effective, and within a few weeks Jennison had his full quota of men. For all of his promises of revenge, the military command was determined to keep him from raiding into Missouri, and the Fifteenth had little to do; however, just the rumors that Jennison was back in Kansas with a regiment ended the Bushwhacker raids.

Author Stephen Starr described Jennison's after-war life.

> After the war, in partnership with his brother "Lon," he owned and operated a three hundred acre stock farm on the Lawrence road, some two miles south of Leavenworth. The farm, located "in the midst of the most beautiful pastoral scenery," was the showplace of the neighborhood. It had "an abundance of good grass and clover, with an inexhaustible supply of water," varied with "a broad panoramic sweep . . . [*of*] teeming grain fields and densely wooded heights." The colonel's peach orchard was famous throughout the state, and so were his pedigreed Durham cattle, his Chester White, Cheshire, and Berkshire hogs, and his large flock of "all the choice breeds of game chickens, viz., Heathwoods, Irish Grays, Jersey Blues and Deserters." But the chief pride of the establishment was Jennison's stud of thoroughbred racehorses and standard-bred trotters, looked after by a trainer and a half-dozen stable hands and exercise boys. One newspaper noted the appropriateness of Jennison's connection with the breeding of racehorses in that "for some five or six years the Colonel enjoyed unusual facilities for selecting fast horses from numerous stables."[44]

The paper was, of course, referring to the many horses stolen through the years by the Jayhawkers.

Charles Jennison died in Leavenworth in 1888 and was buried in Greenwood Cemetery. The Leavenworth *Daily Standard* wrote of the event and accurately described the man who had been a hero to many.

> Thus peacefully ended the career of a man whose violent death has been many times predicted. . . . Charles R. Jennison was no saint. He never professed to be. It was his lot to play a stirring part in troublous times. He loved excitement, disliked restraint and had little reverence of any kind; but in all his turbulent career, he retained qualities which made him popular with men who were his direct opposites in character. . . . He was a man with many faults, but true to a great cause when it needed every helping hand, and now that he is dead, the voice of his friends will be heard and the good he did will be remembered.[45]

*Chapter Two*

# Kansas Territory
# and Its Politics

*E*ARLY IN 1854, hoping to help drive slavery from Kansas, Eli Thayer, of Massachusetts, secured a grant to charter a corporation called the Massachusetts Emigrant Aid Company — later becoming the New England Emigrant Aid Company to be a broader organization. Thayer's plan, backed by a capital of $5 million, was to fill the Kansas Territory with antislavery emigrants and thereby secure Kansas as a free state. Thayer's corporation, and especially his hefty capital, threatened and alarmed the people who lived in the western part of Missouri. These plantation owners held many slaves and feared that large numbers of abolitionist emigrants would induce their slaves to escape and flee to freedom. They also feared that the emigrants would incite blacks

Senator David R. Atchison.
*Kansas State Historical Society, Topeka*

to rise against their white masters, as had happened in the South with Nat Turner. In an attempt to counteract the Emigrant Aid Companies, the proslavery leaders of western Missouri formed secret societies called "The Blue Lodge," "The Social Band," and "The Sons of the South." Two leaders of these proslavery societies were Senator David R. Atchison and Benjamin Franklin Stringfellow. Stringfellow was a well-liked lawyer from Weston, Missouri, a natural leader and supposedly the first person to be called a "Border Ruffian." Governor Andrew Reeder of Kansas gave him the sobriquet "frontier ruffian," and the term eventually evolved into the infamous "Border Ruffian."[1] Stringfellow was supposedly the first person to be called this. Senator Atchison, also from Missouri, claimed the credit for the writing of the Kansas-Nebraska Bill.

. . . One warm day last summer a large crowd had assembled at the town site of Atchison in Kansas to attend the sale of lots. "Dave" himself was there, and as there was much whiskey and many friends, he got "glorious" a little earlier in the day than usual. So with much spitting on his shirt and making himself more nasty than common the Vice President delivered himself something after this wise:

*"Gentlemen, you made a d—d fuss about Douglas, but Douglas don't deserve the credit of this Nebraska bill. I told*

*Douglas to introduce it. I originated it. I got Pierce committed
to it, and all the glory belongs to me.* All the South went for it,
all to a man but Bell and Houston, and who are they? Mere
nobodies, no influence, nobody cares for them."[2]

By the summer of 1854, the Emigrant Aid Company began sending
antislavery settlers into Kansas. The first party, headed by Charles Robinson, founded the town of Lawrence, named for the principal financial
backer of the Emigrant Aid Company, Amos A. Lawrence. Lawrence,
from its foundation, was known as the home of the free-staters.

Charles Robinson was an educated man, as were many of the Emigrant
Aid Company settlers. The New England people were by and large
engaged in professions such as teaching, medicine, and law. They valued
education and encour-
aged the shared gov-
ernment of town meet-
ings. Robinson was
trained as a medical
doctor, but was a clever
and successful busi-
nessman. Motivated by
his desire for leader-
ship and wealth, he
accumulated a fortune,
becoming the most
wealthy citizen of the
state of Kansas in his
time.[3]

Benjamin F. Stringfellow.
*Kansas State Historical Society, Topeka*

Though Charles
Robinson and James
Lane were both free-
staters, they had very
different views and
many times clashed on
issues. Lane, motivated
by political power, and
Robinson, motivated
by the power of wealth,

also had very different personalities. Author William E. Connelly, in his *History of Kansas*, compares the two men:

> Robinson was shrewd, cold, suspicious, calculating. Lane was impulsive, warm-hearted, generous, magnetic. Robinson kept to the office, the farm, the bank and the counting-house. Lane sought the open and the companionship of men. Robinson looked well beyond every transaction, political and otherwise, to the dollar at the other side. He would establish a free State, but he would compel the process to yield him a fortune for his efforts. He was patriotic, but his patriotism was not free from selfish motives. Lane found his recompense in the joys of leadership. His patriotism was not tainted with self-interest. He sought office for the political power it gave him. He was a follower of Jackson, and a spoilsman. He believed in a political organization, a political machine. . . . No two men were ever more directly opposite in temperament, method, the paramount objects of life. Yet Kansas needed both.[4]

Even though Lane was the military man of the two, Robinson was the one with the foresight to request from the New England Emigrant Aid Company a large supply of Sharp's rifles, capable of firing 10 or more shots per minute and able to kill a man at 1,000 yards. All agreed that the Sharp's was the best rifle of the day. These weapons helped to balance the fighting between the Missourians and the out-numbered free-staters. Sharp's rifles later got

Charles Robinson.
*Kansas State Historical Society, Topeka*

the name of "Beecher's Bibles" as the Reverend Henry Ward Beecher roused his congregations to support the settlers and to supply them with Sharp's rifles.

Although Charles Robinson was possibly more subtle than Lane, his strength in the early years was critical to the free-staters' survival. Quieter and more thoughtful than Lane, he was equally solid, as evidenced by his lifelong motto, "Suffer and grow strong."[5] When Kansas became a state in 1861, he was rewarded by his fellow Kansans with the office of Governor.

President Franklin Pierce appointed Andrew H. Reeder Governor of the Territory of Kansas, in June 1854. Reeder was the first in a long line of Governors appointed by a Democratic President sympathetic to slavery. Territorial Governors tended to reflect the political ideas of the President who appointed them and most were biased against the free-staters. Proslavery people, alarmed by the heavy flow of free-staters to Kansas, encouraged Governor Reeder to take a census and order an election. When he did, Atchison and Stringfellow urged Missourians to cross

President Franklin Pierce.
*Kansas State Historical Society, Topeka*

the border and vote for the proslavery candidate, John W. Whitfield. Several hundred armed men responded and crossed into Kansas Territory to vote illegally. When, in March 1855, Reeder called for the election of the Legislature, Atchison and Stringfellow and their secret societies were prepared, and more than 5,000 Missourians armed with weapons and whiskey crossed the border to vote for proslavery candidates.

News of these deeds traveled beyond Kansas and were reported by papers in New York, Chicago, St. Louis, and other cities in the United States. Led by Horace Greeley, founder and editor of the *New York Tribune*, the entire nation was following what was happening in Kansas. Greeley would be the first to use the terminology "Border Ruffians" to designate the proslavery people of western Missouri. He described them as

> . . . savage, ignorant, brutal creatures, with long unkempt hair, unshaven faces and ferocious bearing, roughly clad, with battered hats, frowsy shirts, bowie knives sticking out of boot-tops, revolvers thrust in belts, rifles held menacingly.[6]

On the other hand, Greeley described Northern emigrants

> . . . as well attired, unarmed, intelligent men, of orderly deportment, grave but kindly countenance, industrious, sober, religious, law-abiding.[7]

These sympathetic newspapers assisted their contingents in Kansas by reporting events, however exaggerated, in an effort to appeal to the South or the North to send money and emigrants to Kansas.

The Kansas Legislature, elected under such questionable circumstances, was considered "bogus" by many from the very beginning and was called appropriately the "Missouri-Kansas Legislature." The Legislature proceeded to adopt in total the civil and criminal codes of Missouri, including slavery. Thus was slavery established in Kansas.

The free-staters, however, refused to recognize the new "illegitimate" government and formed a political party called the Free State Party. The Law and Order Party, formed by the proslavery forces, denounced the conduct of the Free State Party as revolutionary and treasonable, and claimed that law and order were the first essentials under any form of government. They called on all citizens, regardless of their views on slavery, to support the government. The Free State Party ignored the regular elections determined by the Legislature and held elections of their own. They chose Mark Delahay as their representative to Congress. Other leaders of the Party were James H. Lane and Charles Robinson.

About this time, Lincoln gave his opinion about the events in Kansas in a letter to his friend Joshua F. Speed:

*Springfield, Aug 24, 1855*

*Dear Speed:*

*You know what a poor correspondent I am. Ever since I received your very agreeable letter of the 22nd of May I have been intending to write you in answer to it. You suggest that in political action now, you and I would differ. I suppose we would; not quite as much, however, as you may think. You know I dislike slavery and you fully admit the abstract wrong of it. So far there is no cause of difference. But you say that sooner than yield your legal right to the slave — specially at the bidding of those who are not themselves interested, you would see the union dissolved. I am not aware that any one is bidding you to yield that right; very certainly I am not. I leave that matter entirely to yourself. I also acknowledge your rights and my obligations, under the constitution, in regard to your slaves. I confess I hate to see the poor creatures hunted down, and caught, and carried back to their stripes, and unrewarded toils; but I bite my lip and keep quiet. In 1841 you and I had together a tedious low-water trip, on a Steam Boat from Louisville to St. Louis. You may remember, as I well do, that from Louisville to the mouth of the Ohio there were, on board, ten or a dozen slaves, shackled to-gether with irons. That sight was a continual torment to me; and I see something like it every time I touch the Ohio, or any other slave-border. It is hardly fair for you to assume, that I have no interest in a thing which has, and continually exercises, the power of making me miserable. You ought rather to appreciate how much the great body of the Northern people do crucify their feelings, in order to maintain their loyalty to the constitution and the Union.*

I do oppose the extension of slavery, because my judgment and feelings so prompt me; and I am under no obligation to the contrary. If for this you and I must differ, differ we must. You say if you were President, you would send an army and hang the leaders of the Missouri outrages upon the Kansas elections; still, if Kansas fairly votes herself a slave state, she must be admitted, or the Union must be dissolved. But how if she votes herself a slave state unfairly—that is, by the very means for which you say you would hang men? Must she still be admitted, or the Union be dissolved? That will be the phase of the question when it first becomes a practical one. In your assumption that there may be a fair decision of the slavery question in Kansas, I plainly see you and I would differ about the Nebraska-law. I look upon that enactment not as a law, but as violence from the beginning. It was conceived in violence, passed in violence, is maintained in violence, and is being executed in violence. I say it was conceived in violence, because the destruction of the Missouri Compromise, under the circumstances, was nothing less than violence. It was passed in violence, because it could not have passed at all but for the votes of many members, in violent disregard of the known will of their constituents. It is maintained in violence because the elections since clearly demand it's repeal, and this demand is openly disregarded. You say men ought to be hung for the way they are executing that law; and I say the way it is being executed is quite as good as any of its antecedents. It is being executed in the precise way which was intended from the first; else why does no Nebraska man express astonishment or condemnation? Poor Reeder is the only public man who has been silly enough to believe that any thing like fairness was ever intended; and he has been bravely undeceived.

That Kansas will form a Slave constitution, and, with it, will ask to be admitted into the Union, I take to be an already settled question; and so settled by the very means you so pointedly condemn. By every principle of law, ever held by any court, North or South, every negro taken to Kansas is free; yet in utter disregard of this in the spirit of violence merely — that beautiful Legislature gravely passes a law to hang men who shall venture to inform a negro of his legal rights. This is the substance, and real object of the law. If, like Haman, they should hang upon the gallows of their own building, I shall not be among the mourners for their fate.

In my humble sphere, I shall advocate the restoration of the Missouri Compromise, so long as Kansas remains a territory; and when, by all these foul means, it seeks to come into the Union as a Slave state, I shall oppose it. I am very loth, in any case, to withold my assent to the enjoyment of property acquired, or located, as good faith; but I do not admit that good faith, in taking a negro to Kansas, to be held in slavery, is a possibility with any man. Any man who has sense enough to be the controller of his own property, has too much sense to misunderstand the outrageous character of this whole Nebraska business. But I digress. In my opposition to the admission of Kansas I shall have some company, but we may be beaten. If we are, I shall not, on that account, attempt to dissolve the Union. On the contrary, if we succeed, there will be enough of us to take care of the Union. I think it probable, however, we shall be beaten. Standing as a unit among yourselves, you can, directly, and in-directly, bribe enough of our men to carry the day — as you could on an open proposition to establish monarchy. Get hold of some man in the North, whose position and ability as such, that he can make the support of your measure — whatever it may be — a democratic party necessity, and the thing is done. Appropos of this, let me tell you an anecdote. Douglas introduced the Nebraska bill in January. In February afterwards, there was a call session of the Illinois Legislature. Of the one hundred members composing the two branches of that body, about seventy were democrats. These latter held a caucus, in which the Nebraska bill was talked of, if not formally discussed. It was thereby discovered that just three, and no more, were in favor of the measure. In a day or two Douglas' orders came on to have resolutions passed approving the bill; and they were passed by large majorities!!! The truth of this is vouched for by a bolting democratic member. The masses too, democratic as well as whig, were even, nearer unanamous against it; but as soon as the party necessity of supporting it, became apparent, the way the democracy began to see the wisdom and justice of it, was perfectly astonishing.

You say if Kansas fairly votes herself a free state, as a christian you will rather rejoice at it. All decent slave-holders talk that way; and I do not doubt their candor. But they never vote that way. Although in a private letter, or conversation, you will express your preference that Kansas shall be free, you would vote for no man for Congress who would say the same thing publicly. No such man could be elected from any district in any slave-state. You think Stringfellow & Co ought to be hung; and yet, at the next presidential election you will vote for the exact type and representative of Stringfellow. The slave-breeders and slave-traders, are a small odious and detested class, among you; and yet in politics, they dictate the course of all of you, and are as completely your masters, as you are the masters of your own negroes.

You enquire where I now stand. That is a disputed point. I think I am a whig; but others say there are no whigs, and that I am an abolitionist. When I was at Washington I voted for the Wilmot Proviso as good as forty times, and I never heard of any one attempting to unwhig me for that. I now do no more than oppose the extension of slavery.

I am not a Know-Nothing. That is certain. How could I be? How can any one who abhors the oppression of negroes, be in favor of degrading classes of white people? Our progress in degeneracy appears to me to be pretty rapid. As a nation, we began by declaring that "all men are created equal." We now practically read it "all men are created equal, except negroes." When the Know-Nothings get control, it will read "all men are created equal, except negroes, and foreigners, and catholics."

*When it comes to this I should prefer emigrating to some country where they make no pretence of loving liberty — to Russia, for instance, where despotism can be taken pure, and without the base alloy of hypocracy.*

*Mary will probably pass a day or two in Louisville in October. My kindest regards to Mrs. Speed. On the leading subject of this letter, I have more of her sympathy than I have of yours.*

*And yet let [me] say I am*

*Your friend
forever*

*A. Lincoln*[8]

Lincoln's pessimism concerning Kansas becoming a free state is clearly understood from this letter. Incidents that had occurred at this point in Kansas history certainly made the possibility of freedom very uncertain. The letter also makes clear Lincoln's repugnance of the treatment of the slaves on the steamboat to St. Louis, an experience that quite probably further fed his antislavery views.

Even though Lincoln abhorred violence and spoke against the violence of John Brown, he would soon come to the conclusion that freedom would not be achieved without bloodshed. Yet he understood that war could not settle the underlying issues. Over 80 years later, February 7, 1940, the *Leavenworth Daily Times* quoted Lincoln:

> Suppose you go to war, you cannot fight always; and when, after much loss on both sides, and no gain on either, you cease fighting, the identical old questions . . . are again upon you.

Wakarusa, a small town three miles from Lawrence, would become the site of the first confrontation between free-staters and proslavery forces. Missourians were threatened by the Topeka Constitutional Convention where free-staters drafted a nonslavery platform. The deliberate killing of a free-stater over a land claim exacerbated the conflict. The free-staters, being fearful of an attack on Lawrence, gathered their forces and prepared to fight. Proslavery forces lined up behind their fortifications and began practicing their cannon fire. Lane took the leader's role for the first time. When the weather turned suddenly cold, Lane endeared himself to his grumbling men by an impassioned speech, as reported by a listener:

> He became afire with eloquence. Off went his large, circular military cloak, next his hat, soon his coat, as he saw his appeal was telling; then his vest followed . . . and his necktie was soon lying with his other clothing upon the ground, his shirt was unbuttoned down the front, while shouts and cheers of applause went up from the men.
>
> Next his shirt-sleeves were unbuttoned and rolled above the elbows, and as he paced, like some wild animal, rapidly back and forth on the embankment, with the perspiration standing in great beads upon his face, notwithstanding it was a sharp December day, he poured forth a stream of eloquence. . . .[9]

Lane convinced his men to stay and fight, but the final storm never came. Even though the Wakarusa War ended without a major battle, it created an ember of hatred for the Missouri ruffians in the soul of newly arrived John Brown. Brown's anger would continue to smolder until it exploded in the Pottawatomie massacre.

Tensions between the proslavery and free-state groups continued to grow and culminated in the first sacking of Lawrence on May 21, 1856, by Missourians and Southern sympathizers — Kickapoo Rangers. Newspaper offices were destroyed, Charles Robinson's house burned, and the town generally pillaged. Hoping to save their town, the free-staters chose a policy of non-resistance and the fighting men left town, leaving behind their terrified women and children.

Newspapers all over the North reported the "sacking of Lawrence," and in Congress, Kansas and its troubles were the main topic of conversation. In response to the situation there, Senator Charles Sumner of Massachusetts, on May 19, 1856, presented an address entitled "Crime Against Kansas." In the speech, he outlined all of the administration's illegal actions in Kansas, the illegal voting of Missourians, and the premeditated violence perpetrated against free-staters in Kansas. Senator Sumner never mediated his language, calling Southern sympathizers ". . . hirelings, picked from the drunken spew and vomit of an uneasy civilization — in the form of men."[10] With the entire gallery roaring in protest, Senator Sumner, not to be dissuaded from his passion, continued by addressing Senator Andrew Pickens Butler from South Carolina, who had advocated the forced disarmament of free-state men:

> The senator from South Carolina has read many books of chivalry, and believes himself a chivalrous knight, with sentiments of honor and courage. Of course he has chosen a mistress to whom he has made vows, and who, though ugly to others, is always lovely to him; though polluted in the sight of the world, is chaste in his sight. I mean the harlot slavery.[11]

Senator Sumner learned the wisdom of Proverbs 15:1, "A mild answer turns away wrath, sharp words stir up anger," as his words created a virtual storm in the gallery. Senator Douglas replied that Sumner's language might "provoke some of us to kick him as we would a dog."[12] The threatened violence was ultimately realized when Representative Preston S. Brooks of South Carolina, a relative of Butler's, attacked Sumner in the Senate chamber two days later. Brooks stepped up to Sumner, who was bowed over his desk writing, and said, "I have read your speech twice over, carefully; it is a libel on South Carolina and Mr. Butler, who is a relative of mine."[13] After speaking, Brooks struck Sumner repeatedly with his gutta-percha cane until it broke and Sumner fell bleeding and unconscious to the floor. Brooks resigned from Congress under heavy protest but was immediately re-elected by approving Southerners who sanctioned his behavior, and, in a sign of approval, sent him dozens of gold-headed canes.

Vicious words and violence were a part of the slavery issue whether one was in Kansas or in Congress.

James Lane, at the direction of the Free State Legislature and Constitutional Convention, went to Washington, D.C., in March 1856 in an endeavor to have Kansas admitted as a state under the Topeka Constitution and to tour the North in the interests of Kansas. The Constitution was presented to the Senate by Michigan Senator Lewis Cass, where it was attacked by Senator Stephen Douglas, forcing Cass to withdraw it. Later, Lane wrote Douglas demanding that he explain a personal allusion to him made by Douglas during the Senate speech. Douglas replied and Lane challenged him to fight a duel. Douglas refused saying that Lane was inferior to him in official rank.[14]

Even though Lane's appeal to Congress was a failure, his tour of the North was very much a success. Lane's magnetic oratorical powers served him well, as he was able to bring in over $15,000 in Chicago alone and supply and raise an army from the North. A. T. Andreas, in his *History of the State of Kansas*, said of Lane's Chicago presentation:

> No man of his time possessed such magnetic power over a vast miscellaneous assembly of men as he. With two possible exceptions (Patrick Henry and S.S. Prentis), no American orator ever equaled him in effective stump-speaking, or in the irresistible power by which he held his audiences in absolute control. On that night he was at his best. It was doubtless the ablest and most effective oratorical effort of his life.

Andreas quotes a portion of Lane's speech.

> I have been sent by the people of Kansas to plead their cause before the people of the North. Most persons have a very erroneous idea of the people of Kansas. They think they are mostly from Massachusetts. They are really more than nine-tenths from the Northwestern States. There are more men from Ohio, Illinois and Indiana, than from all New England and New York combined. . . . The Missourians poured over the border in thousands, with bowie knives in their boots, their belts bristling with revolvers, their guns upon their shoulders, and three gallons of whisky per vote in their wagons. When asked where they came from, their reply was "From Missouri;" when asked, "What are you here for?" their reply was "Come to vote." If any one should go there and attempt to deny these things, or apologize for them, the Missourians would spit upon him. They claim to own Kansas, to have a right to vote there and to make its laws, and to say what its institutions shall be. . . . The Legislature first

passed acts virtually repealing the larger portion of the Constitution of the United States, and then repealed, as coolly as one would take a chew of tobacco, provisions of the Kansas-Nebraska bill. Of this bill I have a right to speak — God forgive me for so enormous and dreadful a political sin — I voted for the bill. I thought the people were to have the right to form their own institutions, and went to Kansas to organize the Democratic party there, and make the State Democratic, but the Missouri invaders poured in — the ballot-boxes were desecrated — the bogus Legislature was elected by armed mobs: you know the rest.

The Pro-slavery fragment of the Democratic party talk much about Knownothingism. It is their song day and night. Well, these Kansas law-makers have gone to work and repealed at once the clause in the Nebraska Bill that gave the right to vote to foreigners in Kansas on declaring their intention to become citizens, and made it requisite for them to have lived in the Territory five years to take the final oath; and at the same time, they made all Indians who adopted the habits of the white men, voters at once. And what was the distinguishing habit of white men? Why, it was understood to be drinking whisky. All that was necessary to naturalize a Kansas Indian was to get him drunk. What Knownothing lodge ever went so far in the nativism as this? — made foreigners in the Territory wait five years to become citizens, and enfranchising the drunken, thieving Indians at once, one and all!

The Pro-slavery fragment of the Democratic party also delights in the term "negro-worshipper," to designate Free-State men. I will show you that these Pro-slavery men are of all negro-worshippers the most abject. According to the Kansas code [Col Lane read from the book giving page and section], if a person kidnaps a white child, the utmost penalty is six months in jail — if a negro baby, the penalty is death. Who worships negroes, and slave negro babies at that? To kidnap a white child into slavery — six months in jail; to kidnap a negro into freedom — death![15]

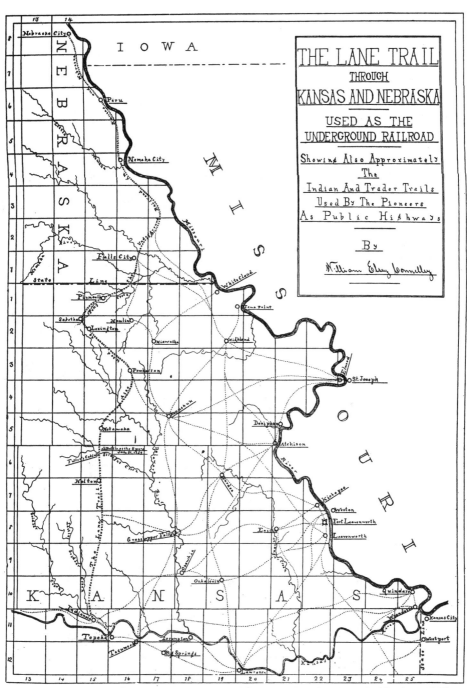

From *History of Kansas State & People*, Vol. 1 (New York: American Historical Society, 1928).

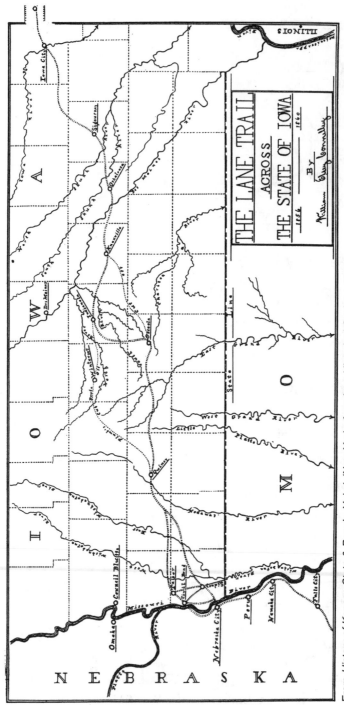

At Buffalo, New York, a general organization was formed for the purpose of aiding the free-state settlers of Kansas. At a meeting held July 9, 1856, a national Kansas committee was appointed. This 17-member group, drawn from free states, included Abraham Lincoln. The purpose of the committee was to collect and distribute to the needy in Kansas contributions of provisions, arms, or clothing. During the six months the committee was in existence, it collected and distributed $120,000, in addition to material goods.

Other Kansas aid societies were formed and were of great assistance to Lane during that summer of 1856 and assuredly helped to win the struggle for freedom in Kansas.[16]

A national organization was formed in the North that responded to Lane's request that a northern route be opened to emigrants to come to Kansas without having to pass through proslavery Missouri where they were harassed. Many were insulted, maltreated, and turned back at blockades on the Missouri River by Border Ruffians.

The one man feared by the Border Ruffians, other than John Brown, was James Lane. He was known from his reputation of bravery during the Mexican War. News of his raising an army in the North sent fear into the hearts of the proslavery forces in Missouri and Kansas. Territorial Governor Daniel Woodson responded by issuing a proclamation forbidding the meeting of the Free State Legislature. From this time on, free-staters became convinced that their only recourse was to fight the Border Ruffians, and guerrilla warfare spread over the territory.

The first step in bringing emigrants and an army through Iowa was the mapping out of a trail; it became known as "The Lane Trail," and would later become the Underground Railroad of Kansas over which hundreds of slaves traveled to freedom in Canada. John Brown directed the use of the trail, and took slaves over it himself. Brown would leave Kansas for the last time over "The Lane Trail" headed for the East and ultimately Harpers Ferry.[17]

By August 1856, Lane's army had avoided the United States troops stationed along the Kansas-Missouri state line to turn them back, Lane's men were responding to the Border Ruffians who had been overrunning the territory murdering and robbing free-staters. On September 1st, the recently elected mayor of Leavenworth, William E. Murphy, expelled every free-state man from town. Free-staters who did not flee — about 150 men, women, and children — were placed aboard a steamboat and ordered to leave. Lawrence was filled with Leavenworth refugees. Others appealed to the military at Fort Leavenworth for protection. But the commander of Fort Leavenworth, Captain Samuel Davis Sturgis, refused protection and asked the free-staters to leave the grounds. Incoming Governor John White Geary was finally able to restore order using the power of the same military that had refused to help fleeing Leavenworthians.

In a period of seven years, between 1854 and 1861, Kansas had 26 executive terms of Governors and Acting Governors.[18] The Governors were appointed for four years, but none of them served a full term. They were either removed by the President, or they resigned due to the pressures of the office. Presidents Franklin Pierce and James Buchanan were both Democratic, with proslavery positions. Consequently, the Governors came into office with a bias toward the proslavery forces, and even if they were sympathetic to the free-staters, they were politically restricted as to the range of their decisions. They could be sure, regardless of any attempts to be fair, that decisions made in favor of one side would instantly be challenged by the other. Decisions made that were opposed to the proslavery forces would be challenged by President Pierce, who was anxious that stories of Kansas' problems not reach Washington, D.C., and the Legislature. And thus, this environment did not lend itself to long gubernatorial terms; the constant turnover added to the already unsettled region.

On the other hand, free-staters knew that the sympathies of the North were their only hope for monies and supplies, and they wanted the story to stay in the ears of the people. Lane had done an outstanding job of keeping Kansas in the minds of the nation through his actions that the papers reported and his very successful personal tour of the North.

The Supreme Court became involved in the slavery issue when, on March 6, 1857, it announced the Dred Scott decision, adding fuel to an already explosive situation. Dred Scott was a negro slave who had been purchased by a U.S. Army surgeon, John Emerson, stationed at Jefferson Barracks in St. Louis. Emerson moved the next year from Missouri, a slave state, to Illinois, a free state. Later he moved to Fort Snelling in the northern part of the Louisiana Purchase. In 1838, Emerson returned to St. Louis with his slave. Dred Scott had meanwhile taken a wife and had become the father of a child. Scott sued for his and his family's freedom on the grounds that his residence in a free territory had made him free.

The court's decision covered three main points:

(1) Negroes were not citizens and therefore could not sue in the federal courts;

(2) a slave's residence on free soil did not make him a free man upon his return to slave territory;

(3) the Missouri Compromise of 1820, which had forbidden slavery in that part of the Louisiana Purchase (except Missouri) lying north of Missouri's southern border, was an unconstitutional exercise of congressional power as it was a violation of the due process of law clause of the 5th Amendment.

Of the nine judges on the Supreme Court, seven were Democrats, and of these, five were appointed from slave states. The decision divided public sentiment even more along party lines, with Democrats and the South accepting and commending, and the North and the Republicans rejecting and condemning it. This decision was also a serious blow to antislavery proponents who wanted to keep slavery out of the territories. It was an issue with runaway slaves who entered free territories like Kansas and constitutionally had to be returned to their masters. It would also become a topic in the Lincoln-Douglas debates.

Lincoln discussed the Dred Scott decision in a speech of May 18, 1858, at Edwardsville, Illinois, showing his pessimism concerning the impact of the decision to move the nation that much closer to a complete slave nation.

> I believe the government cannot endure permanently half slave and half free. I expressed this belief a year ago; and subsequent developments have but confirmed me. I do not expect the Union to be dissolved. I do not expect the house to fall; but I do expect it will cease to be divided. It will become all one thing or all the other. Either the opponents of slavery will arrest the further spread of it, and put it in course of ultimate extinction; or its advocates will push it forward till it shall become

alike lawful in all the States, old as well as new. Do you doubt it? Study the Dred Scott decision, and then see how little even now remains to be done. That decision may be reduced to three points.

The first is that a negro cannot be a citizen. That point is made in order to deprive the negro, in every possible event, of the benefit of that provision of the United States Constitution which declares that "the citizens of each State shall be entitled to all privileges and immunities of citizens in the several States."

The second point is that the United States Constitution protects slavery; as property, in all the United States territories, and that neither Congress, nor the people of the Territories, nor any other power, can prohibit it at any time prior to the formation of State constitutions.

This point is made in order that the Territories may safely be filled up with slaves, before the formation of State constitutions, thereby to embarrass the free-State sentiment, and enhance the chances of slave constitutions being adopted.

The third point decided is that the voluntary bringing of Dred Scott into Illinois by his master, and holding him here a long time as a slave, did not operate his emancipation — did not make him free.[19]

Lincoln's fear was that the next step the Supreme Court might take would be to declare that no state could exclude slavery since the Dred Scott decision, in essence, had said that under the Constitution neither the Congress nor the Territorial Legislature could do it. That is what he was speaking of when he said "how little remains to be done." After Lincoln was elected President, the Dred Scott decision received no respect and, without reversal by the Supreme Court, was utterly disregarded.

In Kansas, the Dred Scott decision encouraged the proslavery proponents who felt themselves assured of the support of not only the Congress but the Supreme Court. This encouragement culminated in the passing of the Lecompton Constitution.

After the Topeka Constitution had been rejected by the Congress, a congressional committee was sent to Kansas to investigate the situation. One of the members was Ohio Republican John Sherman, brother of William

Tecumseh Sherman. The proslavery Judge S. D. Lecompte refused to be intimidated by the committee and issued subpoenas for Charles Robinson, Andrew Reeder, James Lane, and Daniel Anthony to appear before the Grand Jury on charges of treason for their role in forming the Topeka Constitution. Sherman urged Robinson to leave the territory, which he did, but was later captured. Reeder successfully left in disguise. Reeder and Mrs. Robinson spoke of the situation in Kansas on May 29, 1856, at the Illinois convention to organize the Republican Party. Lincoln, who was at the convention and already a Kansas sympathizer, delivered his "lost speech," in which he invited his listeners to unite with him and oppose slave power.

The proslavery forces responded to a failed Topeka Constitution and wrote the Lecompton Constitution, that made slavery a part of the new state's constitution. It provided for the return of fugitive slaves and read, in part, "Free negroes shall not be permitted to live in this State under any circumstances." The constitution also provided that the Legislature should have no power to pass laws emancipating slaves or to prevent emigrants from bringing slaves to the territory. In a move that infuriated free-staters, the constitution stated that voting would endorse "Constitution with slavery," or "Constitution with no slavery," but in any case ". . . the right of property in slaves now in this Territory shall in no manner be interfered with."

When free-staters saw the deception of the document, they refused to vote. On December 21, 1857, 6,226 votes were cast for the constitution with slavery, and 569 for the constitution without slavery. Over 2,000 of the votes for slavery were proved to be fraudulent. The Kansas Territorial Governor, Robert John Walker, went to President James Buchanan to protest the convention that had refused to submit the whole constitution to the people for a fair vote. The President opposed Walker and Walker resigned, as had other Governors who favored the proslavery party but could only go so far in what they considered to be illegal behavior.

The first freely elected Kansas Legislature called for a special election on January 4, 1858, at which time the people were asked to vote for or against the whole document. At this election the proslavery forces refused to vote and 10,226 votes were cast against the constitution and 162 in its favor. In spite of this, on February 2, 1858, President Buchanan presented the Lecompton Constitution to Congress with the recommendation that Kansas be admitted to statehood under it. In the accompanying message, President Buchanan treated the antislavery population of Kansas as in rebellion against lawful authority, recognized the invaders from Missouri as rightfully entitled to form a constitution for the State, and declared Kansas as much a slave state as Georgia or South Carolina.[20]

At this time, Stephen Douglas showed rare courage in opposing President Buchanan and the Democratic Party by stating that Kansas should be allowed to vote for the full document. As Douglas said,

> If Kansas wants a slave-state constitution, she has a right to it; if she wants a free-state constitution she has a right to it. It is none of my business which way the slavery clause is decided. I care not whether it is voted down or voted up.[21]

Douglas stood in the breach in this event, for without his opposition, President Buchanan would have probably been successful in pushing the Lecompton Bill through Congress. Ironically, Douglas' position was the beginning of a break in the Democratic Party that would help Lincoln to secure the presidency in 1860. Through this act, the man who had done so much to oppose Lincoln secured a special place of respect in the hearts of the free-staters.

The Senate voted 33 to 25 to admit Kansas under the Lecompton Constitution, but the House voted 120 to 112 to submit the constitution to the people of Kansas for another popular vote. To overcome the deadlock between the two houses, Congressman William English, of Indiana, and his conference committee, submitted the English Bill. The bill has since been called the "English Swindle," as it was indeed a bribe and threat to the people of Kansas.

> The measure offered Kansas a large grant of government lands, and provided that the Lecompton Constitution should be voted on by the people of Kansas. If a majority voted for acceptance, Kansas should be admitted into the Union under the Lecompton Constitution by proclamation of the President. If the people rejected the offer, then the territory could not be admitted as a State until its population reached the number required for a representative. It was in effect a bribe of land to induce the people to accept the Lecompton Constitution.[22]

On August 2, 1858, a vote under the English Bill was taken in Kansas with 11,300 votes cast "Against the proposition of Congress and admission" and 1,788 "For proposition of Congress and admission." Kansas courageously refused to be bribed. This vote reflects that the free- staters clearly had a majority in Kansas and the struggle for freedom in Kansas was over.

While the Lecompton movement was still in progress, the free-staters proposed the Leavenworth Constitution. This constitution, framed at Leavenworth in a forward-looking move, outlawed slavery and asked

President James Buchanan.
*Kansas State Historical Society, Topeka*

for a vote of universal suffrage that would have included blacks and women. After receiving about 3,000 votes in its favor, it was sent to the Congress, but was never voted on by either house.

The fourth and last convention was assembled on July 5, 1859, in Wyandotte. The Wyandotte Constitution, a compromise that outlawed slavery but did not call for universal suffrage, was passed October 4, 1859. It passed the House but not the Senate, until January 1861, when Jefferson Davis and other Southern Senators left the Senate after their respective states seceded from the Union. On that day, the Kansas Bill was immediately called up by William Seward and passed. It was signed by President James Buchanan on January 29, 1861. Dr. Charles Robinson was inaugurated as Governor of Kansas the same day that Jefferson Davis became president of the Confederate States. On April 12, 1861, Fort Sumter was fired upon, and the Civil War began.

On his journey from Illinois to his March 4th Washington inaugural, Lincoln stopped at Philadelphia, Pennsylvania, on February 22, 1861, to raise a new flag over Independence Hall. The flag bore, for the first time, the 34th star — Kansas. He made these remarks:

> Fellow Citizens: — I am invited and called before you to participate in raising above Independence Hall the flag of our country, with an additional star upon it. (Cheers.) I propose now, in advance of performing this very pleasant and complimentary duty, to say a few words. I propose to say that when that flag was originally raised here it had but thirteen stars. I wish to call your attention to the fact, that, under the blessing of God, each additional star added to that flag has given additional prosperity and happiness to this country until it has advanced to its present condition; and its welfare in the future, as well as in the past, is in your hands. (Cheers.) Cultivating the spirit that animated our fathers, who gave renown and celebrity to this Hall, cherishing that fraternal feeling which has so long characterized us as a nation, excluding passion, ill-temper and precipitate action on all occasions, I think we may promise ourselves that not only the new star placed upon the flag shall be permitted to remain there to our permanent prosperity for years to come, but additional ones shall from time to time be placed there, until we shall number as was anticipated by the great historian, five hundred millions of happy and prosperous people. (Great applause.) With these few remarks, I proceed to the very agreeable duty assigned to me.[23]

The issue of governmental support in Kansas was reversed after Lincoln was elected. Under the Pierce and Buchanan Administrations, the proslavery element had the support of the federal government, but when Lincoln became President the free-state forces were sanctioned and sustained by their own government for the first time. They became the forces that fought for the Union when the Civil War began. Kansas would send a larger percentage of her citizens than any other state to continue the fight for freedom and lost more men in proportion to population than any other state; 61 died for every 1,000 enlisted.

The slavery issue in Kansas ruled society, ruled the Congress, ruled the

Supreme Court, and ruled the Executive Mansion. When one considers the pressures brought to bear by the Democratic Congressmen, the Democratic Supreme Court, the Democratic Presidents, their appointed slavery-sympathetic Governors, and the very intense pressure from the Missouri proslavery forces upon the free-staters, it is amazing that Kansas was brought into the Union as a free state. It was largely because of leaders like Charles Robinson, James Lane, and John Brown, who were less than perfect people, but passionate in their beliefs and willing to keep fighting for the cause. Kansas was clearly pivotal in the political issues of the day. Free-staters were, in essence, fighting not only for Kansas, but ultimately for the Union.

In retrospect, one might say that when it came to slavery, as Kansas went, so went the nation. Lincoln could probably never have been elected and the Civil War might never have begun had Kansas come into the Union as a slave state.

*Chapter Three*

# Lincoln's
# Visit to Kansas

HIS, THEN, was the milieu into which Lincoln came.

In 1858, Abraham Lincoln had just finished the debates with Stephen Douglas, vying for a senatorial seat in Illinois. Even though Lincoln lost the election, he did make his position on slavery known and received national attention for some of his famous statements: "A house divided against itself, cannot stand"; "A nation cannot exist half-slave and half-free"; and "Kansas must be free."

Lincoln's observation concerning Kansas was an important one, for it stated Lincoln's political position on slavery at that time. He believed that slavery must be contained within its Southern borders and not allowed to move into new territories. According to Lincoln, these new territories, which included Kansas, should be declared free states.

Considering the extreme views raging in Kansas at the time, from John Brown on the right, declaring no slavery regardless, to the proslavery forces on the left, wanting slavery at any cost, Abraham Lincoln was, indeed, a political moderate on the issue. After becoming President in 1861, Lincoln's focus was on saving the Union; but as time went on, he came to believe that the only way to save the Union was to free the slaves. This belief would ultimately lead to the writing of the Emancipation Proclamation and the passing of the 13th Amendment.

Lincoln came to Leavenworth at the urging of his friend Mark W. Delahay. Delahay had known Lincoln in Illinois where they had been fellow lawyers and shared similar political ideas. Delahay was also a distant relative, as he was married to Louisiana Hanks, Lincoln's cousin. He was a savvy politician in his own right and believed that Lincoln should make a bid for the presidency.

Delahay and Lincoln exchanged many letters through the years, and in one earlier that year, Delahay invited Lincoln to come and help write the platform for the newly forming Kansas Republican Party, which would replace the Free State Party.

*Leavenworth City Feby 8th 1859*

*Hon A Lincoln*

*Your acceptable favor of Feby 1st is at hand. We think that the middle of may would be quite as long as we ought to defer our organization (say Thursday 19th of may, how would that answer) the Democracy are organized industriously shaping things their best all over the Territory, and they are not without hopes with Gov Medary to direct, who is a plausible leader & one of Great policy and a long experience in party management, we intend to go on and make County organizations, but our Territorial platforms will want your aid in devising the Greatest*

Caution must be used and for success we have to yield prehaps some minor Points — success is of the first importance, elsewhere beside in Kansas — and we think effect will follow our organization in the States; <u>You must come</u>, we shall give you a reception that will be long remembered by you — there is no man now alive that will bring together as large a number of Freemen on Kansas soil as your self — You will be formally invited by a committee, and will be met at the Boat by a committee of arrangements and our military companies amid the Roar of old <u>Kickapoo</u>, [a cannon captured from proslavery forces] an old <u>Pro Slavery trophy</u> taken by the Boys from Kickapoo — when through you can proceed on to Council Bluff and have a good time and see the most beautiful country and the fastest City in the world, this alone is worth a visit; Let me hear from you when ever you can indicate with certainty that you will be able to be with us at the Republican mass Convention. Remember me to Gov Bissell

Very Truly Yours

<u>M W Delahay</u>[1]

Lincoln replied, stating his concern over losing time from his law practice and the extra distance involved in getting to Osawatomie.

M. W. Delahay, Esq                                    Springfield,

My dear Sir                                              March 4, 1859

Your second letter in relation to my being with you at your Republican convention, was duly received. It is not at hand just now, but I had the impression from it that the convention was to be at Leavenworth; but day before yesterday a friend handed me a letter from Judge M. F. Conway, in which he also expresses a wish for me to come; and he fixes the place at Ossawatomie.

Judge Mark W. Delahay. *Kansas State Historical Society, Topeka*

This I believe is off of the river, and will require more time and labor to get to it.

It will push me hard to get there without injury to my own business; but I shall try to do it, though I am not yet quite certain I shall succeed.

I should like to know before coming, that while some of you wish me to come, there may not be others, who would quite as lief I would stay away. Write me again. Yours as ever

A. Lincoln[2]

Delahay wrote back encouraging Lincoln to come and reminded him of the work he had done campaigning for Lincoln in his senatorial race against Douglas.

Alton, Ill. March 15th 1859

Hon A Lincoln

Your favor of March 4th was recd at Leavenworth just before I left for this city. There will be a convention at Leavenworth just before the Ossawattamie one comes off — say two days before, and it would be highly Gratifying to us to have you attend both, but that will be left to your own say of course, the Democrats perhaps would rather you would not be with us, allow me the privaledge of being frank, and I will say then that you have more friends in Kansas and better friends than any living man, and which I would be the last among them that could desire you should injure your business by a visit. Still I must trust that you will reply and say that you will be with us about 16th of May — I spent last summer and fall in Ills and done all I could for you, and wanted you to beat your opponent badly, but I am not quite sure it will turn out after all quite as well for you & our party — I return to Kansas in a day or two —

Very Truly Yours                                    M W Delahay[3]

The National Republican Party had been formed in 1854 to oppose the issue of slavery. The Kansas Party, at Lincoln's urging, also adopted an antislavery platform. On May 14th he wrote Delahay:

> Springfield Ills
> May 14, 1859

M. W. Delahay, Esq

My Dear Sir

I find it impossible for me to attend your Republican convention at Ossawatan [Osawatomie] on the 18th. It would have afforded me much personal gratification to see your fine new country, and to meet the good people who have cast their lot there; and still more, if I could thereby contribute any thing to the Republican cause. You probably will adopt resolutions in the nature of a platform; and, as I think, the only danger will be the temptation to lower the Republican Standard in order to gather recruits. In my judgement such a step would be a serious mistake — would open a gap through which more would pass out than pass in. And this would be the same, whether the letting down should be in deference to Douglasism, or to the southern opposition element. Either would surrender the object of the Republican organization — the preventing the spread and nationalization of Slavery. This object surrendered, the organization would go to pieces. I do not mean by this, that no southern man must be placed upon our Republican National ticket for 1860. There are many men in the slave states for any one of whom I would cheerfully vote to be either President or Vice President provided he would enable me to do so with safety to the Republican cause — without lowering the Republican Standard. This is the indispensable condition of a union with us. It is idle to think of any other. Any other would be as fruitless to the South, as distasteful to the North, the whole ending in common defeat. Let a union be attempted on the basis of ignoring the Slavery *question, and magnifying other questions which the people just now are really caring nothing about, and it will result in gaining no single electorial vote in the South and losing every one in the North. Yours very truly.*

*A. Lincoln*[4]

Even though Lincoln could not attend the Kansas Republican Convention, a man who closely shared his views about the slavery issue and was equally influential did visit. Horace Greeley traveled to St. Joseph, Missouri, on May 15, 1859, on the same Hannibal and St. Joseph railroad — the Great Western Railroad Company — as Lincoln would take in November 1859. Greeley, editor of the *New York Daily Tribune*, had been a very outspoken supporter of the free-state settlers in Kansas and strongly supported Kansas coming into the Union as a free state. His pen had been very effective in helping to secure Kansas' freedom. Greeley was traveling West through Kansas to the gold fields in Colorado and ultimately to California. As he traveled, he wrote articles for the *Tribune*, describing his journey. He planned to arrive in Kansas in time to attend the Republican Convention at Osawatomie on the 18th of May and then continue Westward.

When Greeley arrived in Kansas, it had been raining for several days and he and his party had difficulty traveling because of the swollen, flooding streams, some of which were too dangerous to ford. He described Osawatomie as a village of at most 150 houses, situated in the forks of the Marais des Cygnes and Pottawatomie Rivers. The Convention, which met in the unfinished second floor of the Osage Valley house, was attended by the active participants in the Kansas struggle for freedom — some of whom were Samuel C. Pomeroy, Thomas Ewing, Jr., W. A. Phillips, T. Dwight Thacher, John A. Martin, Mark Delahay, Daniel W. "Web" and Cart Wilder, James McDowell, C. K. Holliday, D. W. Houston, Charles Branscomb, O. E. Learnard, and Albert D. Richardson. James Lane was absent. The shared harmony of the group concerning Kansas freedom was divided upon other questions such as the black man in Kansas. Opinions ranged from giving black men the vote to not allowing black men to even live in the state. There is some disagreement as to how much imput Greeley had during the Convention. After the Convention's work was done, he addressed a crowd of nearly 1,000 from an improvised platform just outside the hotel door. Greeley left the next day to continue his journey West.[5]

Meanwhile, Mark Delahay, not to be dissuaded by Lincoln's refusal to attend the Convention, thought the time was right for Lincoln to try a run for the presidency and encouraged him to come to Leavenworth. (Lincoln, while not without political experience, would probably not be considered qualified as a Presidential candidate today.) He had been a member of the Illinois State Legislature for eight years, had served as a Representative in the U.S. Congress for one term, and had received 110 votes as the nominee for Vice President on the first Republican ticket headed by John Charles Frémont, the explorer and cartographer. Delahay believed that Lincoln could win many states in the next election. He encouraged Lincoln to be bold, in a letter of November 14, 1859:

> . . . (I am Frank and do not intend to flatter you) — But today, if you would only discard a little modesty and not distrust your own *Powers*, and <u>strike boldly</u> and for the next 6 months cease to be a modist man. You are more likely in my Judgment to fill the Bill than any man I can think of — You have always distrusted your own ability too much, the only advantage Douglas ever possessed over you was that of <u>impudence</u>; I have the controll of two leading papers in Kansas, Towit, The Daily Register here (by Dugger) and the State Record at Topeka by Ross. Bros. and I have a claim against the Gazette at Wyandotte for $1800 — and am part owner of the two first papers, if I can see the Effort made properly in Illinois they shall all wheel into line, I will probably be a delegate to the next Convention — and <u>think well on this suggestion</u>, I can if such a determined move is made by your friends in Ills, secure Kansas for you I think — I could certainly do so if you would come <u>right up</u> and made a <u>brief canvass</u> for our *State Ticket*: and Kansas if admitted, will be *Potent* in our Convention. Now cant you come up at once; we will pay your Expenses. . . . "[6]

Delahay, in the same letter, spoke about William H. Seward, Lincoln's possible opponent for the Presidential nomination, and also made one of his many requests for money. According to Mary Delahay's writings, her father had inherited "quite a fortune."[7] He owned a home in town in addition to some acreage in Leavenworth County and, supposedly, at one time owned a steamship. The reason for Delahay asking Lincoln for money is unclear.

> *Your last favor placed me again under obligation to you, and I take this occasion to make the proper acknowledgement; the late Election in New York has gone so nearly against us that it will not sharpen the Prestige of the Hon W. H. Seward any for the Presidency — That Election being the last one in New York before nominations will take place next year; will be referred to as an index of the Strength, or rather weakness of Mr Seward in his own State; by a timely and determined stand by the Press of Illinois for you, as a Western man, and Representative man of the West; The fact also that where you followed Douglas this year his influence was Counteracted by a healthy and large Republican gain; and the fact that you carried the popular vote largely against him last year in Illinois; and the fact that you as an old line Clay Whig (born in Ky) would satisfy the American eliment of the Country and Garrantee us New York and Illinois; and your able championship upon the Tariff question in Illinois years ago, would induce Penna to take you, on trust, upon that question, . . .*
>
> *I have $9000 in Territorial Warrants which I expect will be paid upon our admission; I want to pledge 1 or 2 thousand Dolls of them for the loan of 3 or 4 hundred Dollars (and care nothing about the rate of interest) Can you not obtain and bring with you from some friend that amount to loan me; the security shall be to your entire satisfaction, and it will do me more good than $5000 next May — This is a confidential letter from an old friend who professes to be a Pretty Fair Polatician and meaning Exactly what I write — The Harpers ferry affair*

*doubtless has to some Extent hurt us in New York. Now my friend Cant you get in the Carrs and come to Kansas, and will you not provide for me the loan that I so much need; I can give as security, Notes on Geo E Brown Esq of Alton which will fall due some time in December next if that would be preferred — hoping first to see you in Kansas soon, (But if that is impossible) next that you will write me and that your letter may contain good news I Remain Truly*

*Your Friend*

*M W Delahay*[8]

It doesn't appear that Lincoln responded to Delahay's request for money. Delahay wrote Lincoln again the next day, November 15th, encouraging him to come to Leavenworth and help save the election in Kansas for the Republicans:

*Leavenworth Nov 15th 1859*

*My Dear Sir*

*I transmit herewith an <u>invitation</u> from our leading merchants, Bankers, & business men (of the Republican party of this City) You can probably save us two U.S. Senators and our State Ticket; The Report is this morning that the Democrats have a majority in the Territorial Legislature and Parrott is hard run; You are the man for our people and I <u>trust</u> that you may regard the <u>Exigency</u> as demanding some sacrafice on your Part by accepting this appeal from our friends; Telegraph us, and we will make our Calculations accordingly if you Can Come; Our Election comes off Decr 6th while you will be the Guest of the Republicans of Leavenworth City, I shall Expect you to be at home at my house, and shall consider that settled; if you will come You can at three Points meet a majority of the Republicans of Kansas and can certainly do us <u>much good</u>; To loose Kansas to the Republicans now, would be throwing away much of our <u>Prestige</u> for the future; it would be*

*humiliating indeed, if the Democracy shall at last have the cred-
it of Engineering Kansas into the Union as a Democratic
State. Our Election is far more Important to the Republican
party than, Minnesota or Ohio, in both of which a vast amount
of foreign aid was furnished, while we are totally neglected by
our friends in the States — Your well known devotion to the
Republican Cause assures me that this appeal will not be made
in vain, the trip is now easily made by Rail to St Joseph & by
Boat to this City —*

*Truly your friend*

*M. W. Delahay*[9]

Delahay enclosed a letter signed by 53 merchants, bankers, and businessmen of Leavenworth, asking Lincoln to come:

*At our late Election the Democrats carried this county by a
majority of about one hundred votes, and as we send twelve members to the Legislature, the Delegation from this county may
determine the complixion of our first State Legislature; In view
of your Distinguished services last year and the present contest
just over in Ohio; The fact that we have many Illinoians with
us who have known you long, and are large portion from the other
Western States; and regarding You a Representative man of
the Great West; These considerations alone (while we could
give many others) cause your name to inspire us with the hope
that you will come to our City and make us a Speech, and go to
Lawrence & Topeka and address the Republicans. You can
we feel confident do us much good, hoping that you will accept
this invitation and notify us by Telegraph at any early day
stating when you will leave (if you can comply with our earnest
request) we will try and make Your Expenses light and your
visit agreeable and Your welcome hearty; — Truly Your
friends,*

*PS*

*All who have joined in this invitation, have done it without any display, and it is to be regarded by them, wholly a secret matter. We could just as well had One Thousand Republican names as not, but we presume you perfectly well understand how such think are most properly done — We all want to see you in Kansas — it is of the highest importance that you make the sacrifice to <u>respond</u> to this call of your Kansas friends — Come at the Earliest day possible, and be sure to Telegraph me of your Compliance with this request; You shall never be ashamed of our Kind Greeting*

*Truly Your Friend*

*Delahay*

*PS*

*Remember this is the most <u>important period</u> of your political life, and a Compliance with our wishes will be the best thing of all the good ones you ever done for the Republican Party — Think of <u>it</u> well —* [10]

Lincoln's reply showed not only his willingness to come, but his appreciation to Kansans for their perseverance in a shared cause. The *New York Daily Tribune* would print his 1859 reply to his Kansas supporters in the August 30, 1860, edition:

My Friends in Kansas: It has long been an eager desire of my heart to visit you and your noble land. Old acquaintances assure me that by coming to you at this time I may possibly render a slight service to your country and our common cause. When duty calls I ever strive to obey. Not without detriment to my interests, I therefore waive all personal considerations and gladly place myself at the disposal of the friends of Freedom in Kansas, to whom I feel, in common with my countrymen, an eternal debt of gratitude.

Earlier in the fall of 1859, Lincoln had received and accepted an invitation to speak in New York. He knew that he would be heard there by many important people and it would be covered extensively by the press. This invitation to come to Kansas gave Lincoln a welcome opportunity to try out the speech he would later give in New York. In Kansas he would be relatively free of press coverage and, while it would be a very different audience, the people of Kansas had lived out the issues in a way that made them very knowledgeable. If his speech was well received in Kansas, surely it would be successful in New York.

So it was, that on November 30, 1859, Abraham Lincoln arrived by train in St. Joseph, Missouri, the end of the line, on the new railway from Hannibal, Missouri, completed that year. He had ridden all day in an ordinary coach and arrived late in the afternoon. It was Lincoln's only visit to Kansas; he would never go farther West. The December 1, 1859, *St. Joseph Gazette* — a proslavery Democrat paper — reported Lincoln's coming.

> The Hon. Abe Lincoln of Ill., passed through this city yesterday, on his way to Kansas. . . . The Republicans must be badly frightened when they send for big guns from other States to assist them. Old Abe will be lucky if he succeeds in doing for the Republicans of Kansas what he was unable to do for himself in Illinois — best the democracy.

Lincoln was met by Mark Delahay from Leavenworth, and Daniel "Web" Wilder from Elwood, who was a leader of the Republican Party in Kansas Territory and the editor of the *Elwood Free Press*. The man they met was almost six feet, four inches tall and weighing 180 pounds at his heaviest. Wilder would later describe Lincoln as he looked that day:

> They were legs you could fold up. The knees stood up like the hind joints of a Kansas grasshopper's legs. He wore a hat of stovepipe shape, but made of felt, unglazed, not shining, and needing no brush. The buttons were off his shirt. . . .[11]

Lincoln was very aware of his height and always wanted to compare himself with any other tall man he met to see who was taller. He was never concerned with how he looked, and, in fact, joked about how ugly he was. Stephen Douglas, his opponent in the Lincoln-Douglas debates, once called him two-faced, to which Lincoln replied, "I leave it to my audience. If I had another face, do you think I'd wear this one?"[12]

Lincoln was a great storyteller and was not afraid to make himself the brunt of his own joke. He supposedly told this story. One day he was shaving and as he looked at himself in the mirror, he said, " I must be the ugliest man on the face of the earth. But if I ever meet another man uglier than me I will shoot him on the spot." One day he was walking downtown and said to himself, "There he is, the man uglier than me," so he went home and got his gun and confronted the man. "Sir," he said, "I have sworn if I ever met a man uglier than me, I would shoot him on the spot, prepare to die." The man looked at Lincoln and said, "If you can look me full in the face and swear that I am uglier than you, fire away."[13]

When Lincoln came to Kansas he was clean-shaven. He did not grow a beard until after he was elected. Shortly before the election, he received a letter from Grace Bedell, a young girl from Westfield, New York:

Hon A B Lincoln. Dear Sir,

My father has just home from the fair and brought home your picture and Mr. Hamlin's. I am a little girl only eleven years old, but want you should be President of the United States very much so I hope you wont think me very bold to write to such a great man as you are. Have you any little girls about as large as I am if so give them my love and tell her to write to me if you cannot answer this letter. I have got 4 brother's and part of them will vote for you any way and if you let your whiskers grow I will try and get the rest of them to vote for you. You would look a great deal better for your face is so thin. All the ladies like whiskers and they would tease their husband's to vote for you and then you would be President. My father is a going to vote for you and if I was a man I would vote for you to but I will try and get every one to vote for you that I can. I think that rail fence around your picture makes it look very pretty. I have got a little baby sister she is nine weeks old and is just as cunning as *can be. When you direct your letter dir[e]ct to Grace Bedell Westfield Chatauque County New York. I must not write any more. Answer this letter right off. Goodbye. Grace Bedell.*[14]

Lincoln replied:

*Miss Grace Bedell*

*My dear little Miss.*

*Your very agreeable letter of the 15th. is received. I regret the necessity of saying I have no daughters. I have three sons — one seventeen, one nine, and one seven, years of age. They, with their mother, constitute my whole family.*
*As to the whiskers, having never worn any, do you not think people would call it a piece of silly affection if I were to begin it now? Your very sincere well-wisher. A. Lincoln.*[15]

Whether Lincoln thought it "silly" or not, he took Grace's advice and at age 50 grew whiskers, which he wore until he died. After Lincoln was elected in 1860, he traveled by train to Washington, D.C. The train stopped in Westfield, New York, Grace's hometown. Grace was in attendance and describes the event.

I was at the station with my two sisters and Mr. McCormack, who had escorted us there when the President's train arrived. In my hand was a bouquet of roses, which a neighbor had furnished so that I might give them to the President. The crowd was so large and I was so little that I could not see the President as he stood on the rear platform of his train making his address. But at the end of a short speech he announced,

"I have a little correspondent in this place, and if she is present will she please come forward?"

"Who is it? What is her name?" shouted a number of voices from the crowd.

"Grace Bedell," answered Mr. Lincoln.

Taking my hand, the gentleman who had escorted us to the station made a lane through the crowd and led me to the low platform beside the train. The President stepped down from the car, shook my hand and kissed me.

"You see," he said, indicating his beard, "I let these grow for you, Grace."

The crowd cheered and the President reentered his car. I was so surprised and embarrassed by the President's unexpected conduct that I ran home as fast as I could, dodging in and out between horses and buggies, and once crawling under a wagon. Such was my confusion that I completely forgot the bouquet of roses that I was going to give the great man to whom I had offered such rare advice, and when I arrived home I had the stems, all that remained of the bouquet, still tightly clutched in my hand.

It seemed to me as the President stooped to kiss me that he looked very kind, yes, and sad.[16]

Daniel Webster Wilder.
*Kansas State Historical Society, Topeka*

In 1870, 21-year-old Grace Bedell Billings, along with her husband George, left New York and, like Lincoln, made a trip to Kansas. The Billings came as pioneers to Cloud County, Kansas, and homesteaded land near Delphos. They were friends with James "Wild Bill" Hickok, who was the Marshal of Abilene at the time, and who stayed with the Billings for a few days before leaving the area to join the "Buffalo Bill Wild West Show." Grace lived at Delphos until she died at age

87 in 1936. The letter that Lincoln had written to Grace and had been her prized possession throughout her life, was auctioned by her descendants in 1966 for $20,000.

Daniel Wilder later described the events of Lincoln's November 1859 arrival in St. Joseph.

> Delahay came to Elwood and stayed all night, I suppose. He and I went to St. Joseph the next morning, and way down south to the Hannibal depot (the Hannibal & St. Joe R.R. completed that year) and took Lincoln up town in an omnibus. I took him to a barbershop near the Planters' House and bought for him the New York or Chicago papers at the post-office news-stand.[17]

Lincoln kept up on political events through the reading of newspapers. Even though he had less than a year of formal education, he was a voracious reader, borrowing books wherever he went. He was steeped in the classics and quoted Shakespeare and the *Bible* at great length. He had a wonderful memory and was able to quote long passages of poetry after one reading.

Wilder continues:

> . . . Then the three of us went down to the ferry landing, near the old Robidoux building, and sat down in the dirt, on the bank, waiting for Capt. Blackiston's boat. Mr. Lincoln's talk, sitting on that bank, was of Douglas and Colonel Thomas L. Harris, the famous Illinois Congressman. Mr. Lincoln always spoke kindly, almost tenderly, of his political opponents. On some occasion I asked him about John Calhoun, the first surveyor-general of Kansas and Nebraska, the president of the Lecompton Constitution Convention, and probably the ablest Democratic manager we have ever had in Kansas. Mr. Lincoln spoke of Calhoun in terms of the highest esteem, and with affection. Mr. Calhoun had given him a surveying job, when he was poor, needy and unknown, and the great and good man had never forgotten it. Calhoun did his best, — and that was much,

— to plant slavery in Kansas, but he was not the monster that our papers and speeches pictured him."[18]

Wilder brought up the subject of John Calhoun because he had just died in a mysterious manner on October 13, 1859, six weeks earlier. Calhoun was returning by train to Nebraska City, Nebraska, after a trip to Springfield, Illinois, when he reported feeling ill. Upon arrival in St. Joseph, a physician was called and gave Calhoun medication but he died about two hours later. It was determined that Calhoun had died from a massive dose of strychnine poison. Naturally there were still many unanswered questions about the death — questions that were never answered.[19] Some guessed he had been poisoned by adamant free-staters.

D. W. Wilder continues his story of Lincoln's arrival in Elwood, Kansas, a small town on the western bank of the Missouri across from St. Joseph.

> All sat in the dirt waiting for the ferry-boat; to the Great Western hotel, a large frame building. That night he spoke in the dining room of the hotel; the meeting announced by a man going through the streets pounding a gong.[20]

Wilder had met and gotten to know Lincoln that previous summer when he spent several days in the law office of Lincoln and Herndon in Springfield. Wilder was visiting a friend and classmate from Harvard who was studying law in the Lincoln and Herndon office. There had been considerable discussion while he was there with respect to the choosing of a university for Lincoln's son, Robert. Some contended for a Western institution, others for Harvard. Ultimately, Harvard was chosen. This controversy coming back to his mind, Wilder turned to Lincoln in the omnibus in Elwood and inquired how "Bob" was getting along. According to an interview printed in the *Kansas City Star* on February 11, 1909, D. W. Wilder recalled:

> "He threw back his head and laughed, Mr. Wilder said, "and then, in the high, almost falsetto, voice that used to reach the remotest edges of the crowd, he said: 'Bob went down and was

examined, but failed. Next year he's going to Exeter, N.H., to take some more preparation and try again.' He did try again, Mr. Wilder said, and was admitted at Harvard."

Wilder's friendship with Lincoln would be rewarded when he was appointed as Surveyor General in 1863 upon the resignation of Delahay.

Elwood, Kansas, previously called Roseport, was laid out in 1856 on the western banks of the Missouri River. The town quickly grew and prospered, and was the home of the Great Western Hotel, the largest in the state at 200-feet by 40-feet and three-stories high with its 75 rooms. In July 1859, Elwood boasted of more than 2,000 inhabitants. In the spring of that year, several months before Lincoln arrived, the river eroded the sandy banks to such an extent that many people were forced to move their houses in order to save them. The "mighty Mo" would ultimately take the Great Western, and the town gradually declined and moved away from the river. However, when Lincoln arrived, Elwood was still enjoying its early growing days.

The *Elwood Free Press* reported on December 3, 1859:

> Hon. Abraham Lincoln arrived in Elwood Thursday, December 1. Although fatigued with the journey, and somewhat "under the weather," he kindly consented to make a short speech here. A large number of our citizens assembled at the Great Western hotel to hear him.
>
> Mr. Lincoln was received with great enthusiasm. He stated the reasons why he was unable to make a speech this evening. He could only say a few words to us who had come out to meet him the first time he had placed his foot upon the soil of Kansas. Mr. Lincoln said that it was possible that we had local questions in regard to railroads, land grants and internal improvements which were matters of deeper interest to us than the questions arising out of national politics, but of these local interests he knew nothing and should say nothing. We had, however, just adopted a state constitution, and it was probable that, under that constitution, we should soon cease our

territorial existence, and come forward to take our place in the brotherhood of states, and act our part as a member of the confederation.

"Kansas would be free, but the same questions we had had here in regard to freedom or slavery would arise in regard to other territories, and we should have to take our part in deciding them. People often ask, 'Why make such a fuss about a few niggers?' I answer the question by asking, What will you do to dispose of this question? The slaves constitute one-seventh of our entire population. Wherever there is an element of this magnitude in a government it will be talked about. The general feeling in regard to slavery has changed entirely since the early days of the republic. You may examine the debates under the confederation in the convention that framed the constitution and in the first session of Congress and you will not find a single man saying that slavery is a good thing. They all believed it was an evil. They made the Northwest Territory, the only territory then belonging to the government, forever free. They prohibited the African slave trade. Having thus prevented its extension and cut off the supply, the fathers of the republic believed slavery must soon disappear. There are only three clauses in the constitution which refer to slavery, and in neither of them is the word 'slave' or slavery mentioned. The word is not used in the clause prohibiting the African slave trade; it is not used in the clause which makes slaves a basis of representation; it is not used in the clause requiring the return of fugitive slaves; and yet, in all the debates in the convention the question was discussed and slaves and slavery talked about. Now, why was this word kept out of that instrument, and so carefully kept out that a European, be he ever so intelligent, if not familiar with our institutions, might read the constitution over and over again and never learn that slavery existed in the United States? The reason is this: The framers of the organic law believed that the constitution would outlast slavery, and they did not want a word there to tell future generations that slavery had ever been legalized in America.

"Your territory has had a marked history — no other territory has ever had such a history." There had been strife and bloodshed here; both parties had been guilty of outrages; he had his opinions as to the relative guilt of the parties, but he would not say who had been most to blame. One fact was certain — there had been loss of life, destruction of property; our material interests had questions — the way adopted by government until a recent period. The bloody code has grown out of the new policy in regard to the government of territories.

Mr. Lincoln, in conclusion, adverted briefly to the Harper's Ferry affair. He believed the attack of Brown wrong for two reasons. It was a violation of law; and it was, as all such attacks must be, futile as to any effect it might have on the extinction of a great evil.

"We have a means provided for the expression of our belief in regard to slavery — it is through the ballot box — the peaceful method provided by the constitution. John Brown has shown great courage, rare unselfishness, as even Governor Wise testifies. But no man, North or South, can approve of violence and crime." Mr. Lincoln closed his brief speech by wishing all to go out to the election on Tuesday and to vote as became the free men of Kansas.

The next morning, December 1st, Delahay and Wilder put Lincoln in an open carriage (which is on display at the Fort Leavenworth Museum) and took him on to Troy. As they proceeded to Troy, the weather turned unseasonably cold, as it is wont to do in Kansas, and Lincoln was unprepared with a proper overcoat. Along the way they met Henry Villard, an Eastern correspondent, who had met Lincoln during the Lincoln-Douglas debates in Illinois. Villard described his meeting with Lincoln in Illinois.

He and I met accidentally, about nine o'clock on a hot, sultry evening, at a flag railroad station about twenty miles west of Springfield, on my return from a great meeting at Petersburg in Menard County. He had been driven to the station in a buggy and left there alone. I was already there. The train that we intended to take for Springfield was about due. After vainly waiting for half an hour for its arrival, a thunderstorm compelled us to take refuge in an empty freight-car standing on a side track, there being no buildings of any sort at the station. We squatted down on the floor of the car and fell to talking on all sorts of subjects. It was then and there he told me that, when he was clerking in a country store, his highest political ambition was to be a member of the State Legislature. "Since then, of course," he said laughingly, "I have grown some, but my friends got me into this business [*meaning the canvass*]. I did not consider myself qualified for the United States Senate, and it took me a long time to persuade myself that I was. Now, to be sure," he continued, with another of his peculiar laughs, "I am convinced that I am good enough for it; but, in spite of it all, I am saying to myself every day: 'It is too big a thing for you; you will never get it.' Mary insists, however, that I am going to be senator and President of the United States, too." These last words he followed with a roar of laughter, with his arms around his knees, and shaking all over with mirth at his wife's ambition. "Just think," he exclaimed, "of such a sucker as me as President?"[21]

In 1859, Villard, representing the Cincinnati *Commercial*, was the only passenger in the first stagecoach from Fort Leavenworth to Denver. On his return trip to the East in a two-horse wagon with two companions, he had the following encounter on a December day in Kansas:

About thirty miles from St. Joseph an extraordinary incident occurred. A buggy with two occupants was coming toward us over the open prairie. As it approached, I thought I recognized one of them, and, sure enough, it turned out to be no less a person than Abraham Lincoln! I stopped the wagon, called him by name, and jumped off to shake hands. He did not recognize me with my full beard and pioneer's costume. When I said, "Don't you know me?" and gave my name, he looked at me, most amazed, and then burst out laughing. "Why, good gracious! you look like a real Pike's-Peaker." His surprise at this unexpected meeting was as great as mine. He was on a lecturing tour through Kansas. It was a cold morning, and the wind blew cuttingly from the northwest. He was shivering in the open buggy, without even a roof over it, in a short overcoat, and without any covering for his legs. I offered him one of my buffalo robes, which he gratefully accepted. He undertook, of course, to return it to me, but I never saw it again. After ten minutes' chat, we separated. The next time I saw him he was the Republican candidate for the Presidency.[22]

So it was that Abraham Lincoln came into Kansas wrapped in a buffalo robe, which seems somehow appropriate. According to local lore, Lincoln was escorted into Troy by Henry Boder, Judge J. B. Maynard, Joseph Hayton, and John Frank Kotsch. Troy, the only town Lincoln visited not situated on the Missouri River, was plotted in 1855 at the urging of the Territorial Legislature. Riverside locations were ideal because steamboats were not only the communication link with the outside world, but the means by which towns received goods and settlers. The Legislature chose the geographical center of Doniphan County and made Troy the county seat. Supposedly, Lincoln went to the Smith Hotel and stagecoach stop to eat, where he asked for and ate several helpings of "Johnny cakes." He then walked across the street to the one-story courthouse to make his speech.[23]

Albert D. Richardson, a correspondent of the *New York Daily Tribune*, reported on Lincoln's speech at Troy.

> Late in the autumn of 1859, he visited the territory for the first and last time. With Marcus J. Parrott, delegate in Congress, A. Carter Wilder, afterwards representative, and Henry Villard, a journalist, I went to Troy, in Doniphan county to hear him. In the imaginative language of the frontier, Troy was a town — possibly a city — but, save a shabby frame courthouse, a tavern, and a few shanties, its urban glories were visible only to the eye of faith. It was intensely cold. The sweeping prairie wind rocked the crazy buildings, and cut the faces of travelers like a knife. Mr. Wilder froze his hand during our ride, and Mr. Lincoln's party arrived wrapped in buffalo robes.
>
> Not more than forty people assembled in that little barewalled court-house. There was none of the magnetism of a multitude to inspire the long, angular, ungainly orator, who rose up behind a rough table. With little gesticulation — and that little ungraceful — he began, not to declaim, but to talk. In a conversational tone he argued the question of slavery in the territories, in the language of an average Ohio or New York farmer.

I thought "If the Illinoisans consider this a great man their ideas must be very peculiar." But in ten or fifteen minutes I was unconsciously and irresistibly drawn by the clearness and closeness of his argument. Link after link it was forged and welded, like a blacksmith's chain. He made few assertions, but merely asked questions: "Is not this true? If you admit that fact, is not this induction correct?" Give him his premises, and his conclusions were inevitable as death.

His fairness and candor were very noticeable. He ridiculed nothing; burlesqued nothing; misrepresented nothing. So far from distorting the views held by Mr. Douglas and his adherents, he stated them with more strength probably than any one of their advocates could have done. Then, very modestly and courteously, he inquired into their soundness. He was too kind for bitterness, and too great for vituperation.

His anecdotes, of course, were felicitous and illustrative. He delineated the tortuous windings of the democracy upon the slavery question from Thomas Jefferson down to Franklin Pierce. Whenever he heard a man avow his determination to adhere unswervingly to the principles of the Democratic Party, it reminded him, he said, of a "little incident in Illinois." A lad, ploughing upon the prairie, asked his father in what direction he should strike a new furrow. The parent replied, "Steer for that yoke of oxen standing at the further end of the field." The father went away, and the lad obeyed. But just as he started the oxen started also. He kept steering for them, and they continued to walk. He followed them entirely around the field, and came back to the starting-point, having furrowed a circle instead of a line.

The address lasted an hour and three-quarters. Neither rhetorical, graceful, nor eloquent, it was still very fascinating. The people of the frontier believed profoundly in fair play, and in hearing both sides; so they now called for an aged ex-Kentuckian, who was the heaviest slaveholder in the territory; responding, he thus prefaced his remarks: "I have heard, during my life, all the ablest public speakers, all the eminent statesmen of the past and the present generation, and while I dissent utterly from the doctrines of this address, and shall endeavor to refute some of them, candor compels me to say that it is the most able — the most logical — speech I ever listened to."[24]

Colonel Andrew A. Ege was the slaveholder referred to by Richardson, who replied to Lincoln's speech — he would, at a later date, be asking for a favor of President Lincoln. At the conclusion of the speech, Lincoln proceeded to the dry-goods store located at the corner to purchase a pair of overshoes. He bought the largest pair the merchant had in stock — size 13. He walked down the street to a well, where he took a drink of water, and then entered the carriage that would take him to Doniphan.[25]

In 1854, the organizers of the Doniphan Town Company met for the first time to choose a spot for the new town that was known by boatmen as the ideal place for a steamboat to land. Doniphan was named for General Alexander William Doniphan who fought in the Mexican War. The prosperity of the town was quickly enhanced in 1857 by the location of the government land office. In that same year, James H. Lane was made president of the town company.

Lane, who aroused extreme feelings in those who knew him, was the subject of a local story.

> One day, late in the [*1850s*], James Eylar, who lived near Doniphan, while on his way to Atchison in a wagon, overtook a tall, angular man who asked permission to ride with him. As they rode Eylar told the man of some relatives he had living in Missouri, where he had been visiting. "What do you think of Jim Lane, over there?" asked the tall, angular man of Mr. Eylar. "They don't think much of him," replied Mr. Eylar, adding "if they had the blank of a blank over there they would soon hang him." On his arrival in Atchison, Mr. Eylar discovered that he had been riding with the "grim chieftain" himself.[26]

A local citizen described the town of Doniphan in *Redpath's Handbook of Kansas Territory*, published in 1859:

Doniphan, it is admitted by every one, has the best rock-bound landing, and the best townsite on the Missouri river anywhere above St. Louis. It has running through it a fine stream of water, which by a trifling outlay which will soon be expended, can be made to flow through five of the principal streets. A wealthy company has been chartered for the construction of a railroad for St. Joseph, through Doniphan, for Topeka, connecting the Kansas and Missouri rivers. The stock is subscribed — ten per cent paid in. That part of it from St. Joseph to Doniphan will be completed as soon as the connection is made with Hannibal. Lots can be purchased at Doniphan on more liberal terms than at any other town on the Missouri. We say to the emigrant, come to Doniphan; believing as we do, that it is destined to be the great emporium of the upper Missouri. The population is about one thousand.[27]

Lincoln was driven the 18 miles south to Doniphan by his friend, W. H. Nesbitt, a prominent Republican. Upon arrival at the hotel, Lincoln found there were no vacant rooms. Mrs. Julia Elizabeth Boyington and her mother, who were staying at the hotel for the night, volunteered their room to him, and they slept on a pallet in the office.[28]

Ashael Lowe was the owner of the hotel in Doniphan, which was a station on the Underground Railroad and, at one time, had been the headquarters for James Lane. Lowe's 14-year-old son, J. W. Lowe, laid the fire in Lincoln's room and spent two hours with him. When Lincoln asked about the Underground Railroad, J.W. knew all about it, for he had seen a good many runaway slaves. He shared with Lincoln how the slaves were brought there in a wagon by Jack Seelover, a club-footed liveryman, and told how they looked and what they said. The slaves were then taken to Falls City, Nebraska, which was the next station on the Underground Railroad.[29]

According to D. W. Wilder and Lincoln himself, he spoke at the hotel in Doniphan but no one reported what he said. The next morning, December 2nd, Lincoln was escorted to Atchison by Albert D. Richardson, newspaperman from the *New York Daily Tribune*. Upon his arrival, about 10:00 a.m., a handbill was hurriedly put in type and printed in the office of *Freedom's Champion* by Frank A. Root, the foreman. The bill read:

HONEST
ABE
LINCOLN
of Illinois
Will Speak at the
METHODIST CHURCH TO-NIGHT
at 8 o'clock
on the
POLITICAL ISSUES OF THE DAY!
The Public is Invited.
By order of Committee.
Atchison, K.T., Dec. 2, 1859.[30]

Root describes the event:

I remember distinctly the time when Lincoln came to Kansas and visited Atchison; also several of the incidents associated with that visit. It had been a nice warm day, following which was a clear, beautiful moonlight night, the atmosphere a little cool, but by no means uncomfortable, but not warm enough for an outdoor meeting.

Mr. Lincoln, while repairing to the place for speaking, was seated in a carriage with the committee in charge. On the way he was preceded by Atchison's first brass band, led by the pioneer, Lemuel Spooner. From the sightly location of the church it was plainly seen that a goodly portion of the audience represented the cultured and more intelligent classes of opposite political views.

The church, which had been dedicated by the Rev. H. D. Fisher a little more than six months previous, stood near the brow of the hill, where a fine view was had. From the house of worship there were also visible in every direction, numerous groves of hazel brush besides many clusters of small scrub oaks. The meeting was attended by the largest gathering that had ever assembled at this place of worship. There was not even standing room inside for the members of the band, hence they had to listen outside.

The meeting was called to order and the noted speaker was introduced by Hon. S.C. Pomeroy, afterwards chosen one of the first United States senators from Kansas. As Mr. Lincoln arose from his seat on the rostrum, at first many seemed much disappointed in him. But this was owing, no doubt, to the rather uncouth appearance he presented. The hasty opinions, which many had formed of the great man, were soon changed. It was only a little while after Mr. Lincoln began his talk until the audience, almost to a man, realized that it had been mistaken in its hurried and previous estimation formed of the noted speaker, then almost unknown in Kansas. Most of the listeners were shortly convinced that they were not only being entertained by the plain "Honest" Abe Lincoln, but found that he was a man possessed of vast information and far advanced opinions and ideas — one of the ablest men then in the great middle-west, an orater of renown — in short, one of the wisest and most profound minds the nation had ever produced.

For more than two hours and a quarter the famous Illinois "rail-splitter," in language so plain and so simple that a child could understand, addressed the closely packed audience. The speech was conservative. Not one word was spoken that even the most ultra pro-slavery man could take exception to.

Many of those outside the church crowded up as closely as they could to the windows, thinking that they might see the face of the man whose clear ringing voice they were so earnestly listening to. Every one seemed anxious to get a glimpse of the great orator. They were eager to listen to the noble truths that came from his lips. Two or three times during his address the speaker looked at his watch and suggested that perhaps he was speaking too long, but the audience, which by this time practically had become electrified by his remarks, yelled from all parts of the house, "go on, go on!"

Some one asked, "What about old John Brown?" Mr. Lincoln said that only a few hours ago he had heard that "Brown" had been hung, "and," he added, "he ought to have been hung." The old Kansas pioneer of Osawatomie renown had paid the

penalty for operating his "underground railroad" and attempting to establish an important way station along the line at
Harper's Ferry, openly violating the laws of the Old Dominion.
The exciting news of Brown's execution had only a little while
before the meeting began reaching eastern Kansas by telegraph.

Speaking of the new territory that only a few years before
had been thrown open for settlement, the speaker found it necessary to quote a distinguished Kansan and leading citizen of
Atchison who was an attentive listener — General Benj. F.
Stringfellow, a native of Virginia, and who, remarked the
speaker, had given his opinion why "Kansas could never be a
free state," the main reason the general had given, being, said
Mr. Lincoln, "that no white man could break prairie." As he
spoke these words, which instantly brought down the house, it
was noticed that the famous "rail-splitter" had a broad smile on
his countenance, but he quickly remarked that if this were true,
he had been wondering whether or not he himself was a negro,
for he had many times broken prairie.

From first to last the speech was a masterly effort. It was off-
hand, but I never before nor since listened to such a profound
address. For two hours and twenty minutes he held that audience of Kansas pioneers, but it seemed that the time never
passed so quickly. The speaker had something new and interesting to say. His talk was as eloquent as it was sound and logical; as forceful as it was straightforward, loyal and convincing.
The way it was delivered won for the speaker the admiration of
all who heard it, irrespective of party.

At the close of the meeting Mr. Lincoln was escorted back to
the hotel by the band, followed by a goodly portion of the
crowd. In the parlors of the Massasoit he was the center of
attraction among leading free-state men of the town, and a
sprinkling of the more prominent pro-slavery citizens who had
called at his headquarters to pay their respects.

During the conversation that followed some one among the
party, while attempting to illustrate an incident that happened in
the adjoining territory north, had occasion to speak the name of
"Weeping Water," a stream coursing through Nebraska. This

stream was something new to Mr. Lincoln, a name of a creek that he had never before heard of. The occasion appeared to be an opportune time for Lincoln to spring another of his latest jokes. Almost in a twinkling, after hearing the odd name of the stream, he said that if "Minnehaha" meant "laughing water," one might naturally infer that "Weeping Water" meant "Minne Boo-hoo."[31]

Atchison, at this time, had about 2,500 inhabitants. The town was named for Senator David R. Atchison of Missouri, who spent a considerable part of his time there but never made it his legal residence. Atchison had been settled in 1854 by proslavery advocates and was the rival of Leavenworth. But unlike Leavenworth, it continued to be intensely proslavery and was considered the headquarters of the "Border Ruffians" in Kansas. By 1859, the free-state men had not only won the fight for a free Kansas, but had overcome Atchison also. Horace Greeley described Atchison on his trip in May 1859.

> Atchison gives me my first foothold on Kansas. It was long a Border-Ruffian nest, but has shared the fortunes of many such in being mainly bought out by Free-State men, who now rule, and for the most part own it. For the last year, its growth has been quite rapid; of its four or five hundred dwellings, I think, two-thirds have been built within that period. The Missouri at this point runs further to the west than elsewhere in Kansas; its citizens tell me that the great roads westward to Utah, &c., from St. Joseph on the north and from Leavenworth on the south, pass within a few miles of Atchison when thrice as far from their respective starting-points. Hence the Salt Lake mail, though made up at St. Joseph, is brought hither by steamboat and starts overland from this place; hence many trains are made up here for Laramie, Green River, Fort Hall, Utah, and I hear even for Santa Fe. I have seen several twelve-ox teams, drawing heavily-loaded wagons, start for Salt lake, etc., to-day; there are others camped just outside the corporate limits, which have just come in; while a large number of wagons form a corral (yard, inclosure or encampment) some two miles westward. A little further away, the tents and wagons of parties of

gold-seekers, with faces set for Pike's Peak, dot the prairie; one of them in charge of a grey-head who is surely old enough to know better. Teamsters from Salt Lake and teamsters about to start, lounge on every corner; I went out three or four miles on the high prairie this afternoon, and the furtherest thing I could see was the white canvas of a moving train. I have long been looking for the West, and here it is at least — But I must break off somewhere to prepare for an early start for Leavenworth and Lawrence to-morrow, in order to reach Osawatomie next day in season to attend the Republican Convention which is to assemble at that place on Wednesday, the eighteenth.[32]

Lincoln spoke at the Methodist Church that stood on the hill at Fifth and Parallel Streets, the first church erected in the city, having just been dedicated in May 1859. It is said the church was also notable because the Reverend Milton Mahin, a staunch Union Man, was the first minister in Atchison to raise the Stars and Stripes over his house of worship and defy the Southern sympathizers.[33]

Lincoln was introduced by Mayor Samuel C. Pomeroy, who would join James Lane in becoming one of the first two Kansas United States Senators. Pomeroy, unlike Lane, was not a Lincoln supporter, but rather a consistent enemy who would campaign for William Seward in the Presidential election. Even after Lincoln was elected, Pomeroy worked against him, and in February 1864, he published an open letter called the "Pomeroy Circular" that suggested Lincoln should not be re-elected but that the Republican Party should nominate Secretary of the Treasury Salmon Chase for its Presidential candidate.

Senators Lane and Pomeroy hated each other intensely and wrangled persistently over the patronage for their state. Lincoln, impatient with their squabbling over the appointment of an Assessor in Kansas, later refused an interview with Pomeroy and then wrote to him:

> *I did not doubt yesterday that you desired to see me about the appointment of Assessor in Kansas. I wish you and Lane would make a sincere effort to get out of the mood you are in. It does neither of you any good — it gives you the means of tormenting my life out of me, and nothing else.*[34]

Other recognized people attending the Atchison speech were General Benjamin F. Stringfellow, the foremost proslavery leader of Kansas; John J. Ingalls, who later would represent Kansas in the United States Senate for 18 years; Frank A. Root, an Atchison printer; and Franklin G. Adams, first Secretary of the State Historical Society, who would later write his remembrances of that day:

> I had first seen Mr. Lincoln and heard him talk in Atchison in 1859. He was not then popularly known in Kansas. He was known to be a candidate for the nomination in 1860 as president. The people of Kansas were for Wm. H. Seward. Seward had fought our battles in the United States senate. He was the idol of our people; yet Lincoln was greatly admired for his noble defense of our free-state cause in his great debate with Douglas in 1858. In Atchison we appointed a committee to receive him and to provide a place for his address in the evening. He was taken to our best hotel, the Massasoit House, and a good many of the citizens came into the hotel office to shake hands with him and to hear him talk. He was soon started, with his chair tipped up, and among the first to engage in conversation with him was Col. P.T. Abell, the head and brain of the proslavery party in our town and largely in the territory. Both had been Kentuckians. Abell knew many citizens of Illinois who had moved there from Kentucky. The two immediately found mutual acquaintances about whom they could converse, and Lincoln began to tell stories, relating incidents in the lives of Illinois Kentuckians.
>
> I was on the committee to provide a place for the Lincoln meeting that evening. Judge P.O. Wilcox was a member of the committee. The best audience room in town was that of the Methodist church. Our committee hunted up the trustees, and Wilcox says he had considerable difficulty in gaining consent to have a political meeting in a church. I scarcely remember how it was, but Wilcox says we met with such a rebuff and refusal that he lost his patience, and it took the best I could do in the way of persuasion to get the church, which we did. I still remember the appearance of Mr. Lincoln as he walked up the aisle on entering the church and took his place on the pulpit

stand. He was awkward and forbidding, but it required but a few words for him to dispel the unfavorable impression, and he was listened to with the deepest of interest by every member of the audience.

I have mentioned the attachment of the people of Kansas for Wm. H. Seward. Our own local paper, the Atchison Champion, of which John A. Martin was the editor, made no mention of Mr. Lincoln's presence in Atchison at the time. Martin was wrapped up in Seward and could not brook the thought of any encouragement of countenance given by the people of Atchison to a rival candidate.[35]

Senator John Ingalls also reported on the event:

The next day, which was the day of the execution of old John Brown in Virginia, the 2d of December, 1859, I think he came to Atchison, where I then lived and still live, and was received by a committee of citizens. He stopped at the Massasoit house and was announced for a speech in the evening at the Methodist church. It was a bitter cold winter's day, and he made a speech of extraordinary power, in which he anticipated very largely the line of argument he employed a few months later in his celebrated speech in Cooper institute in New York, and made a profound impression upon the people who were assembled to hear him, although his reputation at that time had only been derived from a knowledge that had preceeded him of his debate with Stephen A. Douglas in 1858. Alluding to the threats of the South to secede, Lincoln declared that any attempt at secession would be treason; and none who heard him can forget the impressive majesty of his appearance as he drew himself up and, leaning forward with his arms extended until they seemed to reach across the small auditorium, said, "If they attempt to put their threats into execution we will hang them as they have hanged old John Brown to-day." One of the leading border ruffians declared that it was the most powerful presentation of Republican doctrine that he had ever heard.

Lincoln remained in Atchison until the next day about noon and the committee appointed to entertain him, upon going down to the hotel next morning after breakfast, found him in the bar room by a red hot box stove, engaged in telling jokes and yarns and stories to a crowd of overland stage drivers and other rough characters of the frontier, who received his narrations with the most boisterous and inextinguishable laughter. He exhibited there, as always, an extraordinary facility for forming personal relations with all classes of men. Think of him sitting there with one rubber shoe on and the other unbuckled on his knee for probably half an hour, the carriage waiting outside to take him about the town, while he entertained the crowd with his inexhaustible fun amid bursts of uproarious laughter![36]

An article that appeared in the *Kansas City Journal*, entitled "Beat Lincoln at Billiards," relates this interesting incident.

When Abraham Lincoln visited Atchison in 1859, he stopped at the Massasoit House kept by the late Thomas Murphy. After Lincoln delivered his speech at the old Methodist Church, he went back to the hotel, and played billiards with the landlord. Several years later when Lincoln was president, Thomas Murphy was appointed superintendent of Indian affairs for Kansas and Indian Territory. The appointment was presented to Lincoln by Senator Pomeroy. "Who was Murphy?" Lincoln asked. Pomeroy told him he was the proprietor of the Massasoit hotel in Atchison, Kansas. "Oh," Lincoln said, "is that the little Irishman who beat me playing billiards when I was in Atchison?" The story is told by John B. Murphy, son of Thomas Murphy.[37]

Horace Greeley, during his visit to Kansas, traveled the same route as Lincoln, except he took a steamer from St. Joseph to Atchison where he, too, stayed at the Massasoit. Twelve or fifteen miles from Atchison, Greeley and his party struck the California Trail and followed it south and east into Leavenworth. He described the wagon trains of emigrants on the road:

As we neared the California trail, the white coverings of the many emigrant and transport wagons dotted the landscape, giving the trail the appearance of a river running through great meadows, with many ships sailing on its bosom. Most of the independent wagoners were still encamped by the wayside, unable or unwilling to brave the deep mud; their cattle feeding on the broad prairie; the emigrants cooking or sitting beside the wagons; women sometimes washing, and all trying to dry their clothing, drenched and soaked by the pouring rain of the past night. One great wagon-train was still in corral with its cattle feeding and men lounging about; the others might better have been as it was clearly impossible to make their lean, wild-looking oxen (mainly of the long-horned stripe, which indicates Texas as their native land, and which had probably first felt the yoke within the past week) draw them up the slightest ascent through the deep, slippery mire. A great deal of yelling, beating, swearing, was being expended to little purpose, as I presume each train corraled for the ensuing night within a mile of the point it left in the morning. These contractors' wagons are very large and strong, each carrying a couple of good extra axles lashed under its body, to be used in case an old one gives way under a heavy jerk; the drivers are as rough and wild-looking as their teams, though not quite so awkward at their business; but to keep six yoke of such oxen in line in the road, and all pulling on the load, is beyond human skill. It is a sore trial to patience, that first start of these trains on their long journey — to Utah, Fort Hall, Green River, and some of these to New Mexico though this is not the Santa Fe trail. The loads are generally fifty hundred weight; the wagons must weigh at least fifteen hundred each; and though this would seem moderate for twelve oxen, it must be remembered that they are at this season poor and at first unbroken, and that the road is in spots a very bad one. A train consists of ten to thirty wagons; each train has its reliable and experienced master of director; and when a team is stalled, another is unhitched from its own wagon and sent to the aid of the one in trouble. The rate of progress is necessarily snail-like; these trains will do very well if they make twenty miles the first week; considering the weather. But then the feeding of the teams (like the lodging of the men) costs nothing, as they live on the broad prairie, and though they will often be fearfully hungry or dry in traversing grassless tracts on their route, they are said generally to gain in flesh (for which there is ample room) during a journey of three or four months. Of course, they improve in docility and effectiveness, being at first so wild that, in order to be yoked, they have to be driven into the corral (formed, as I may have explained, by wagons closely ranged in hollow square, the tongue of each being run under its next neighbor, for defense against Indians or other prowlers.) Very few wagons or cattle ever come back; the freighting is all one way; and both wagons and cattle are usually sold at or near their point of destination for whatever they will fetch — to be taken to California or disposed of as they best may.[38]

Greeley visited Leavenworth twice, once on his way to the Osawatomie Convention and once on his way back. During Lincoln's visit, the *New York Daily Tribune* reporter who covered the event noted in the edition of August 30, 1860, Lincoln's humbleness and willingness to speak in small towns:

It will be remembered that up to this time Mr. Lincoln had visited none but "country towns." At no place did his audience exceed 200; but his speeches were always as clear, elaborate, logical, and eloquent, as when he appeared in your mighty metropolis, in an institute thronged with intellect, grace, and power. He paid the kindest deference to all inquiries, and seemed gratified at any interruptions that indicated interest in his "talk," as he was pleased to term his able and eloquent efforts. "I never stop to inquire," said Mr. Lincoln, "as to the character or numbers of those likely to hear me. To accomplish a little good is more gratifying to me than to receive empty applause." It was in this spirit he met the farmers and mechanics of Kansas, and they returned for it the homage of interest, affection, and confidence.

The *New York Tribune* went on to describe the preparations made in Leavenworth for Lincoln's arrival:

Leaving Mr. Lincoln's carriage jolting over the hard clods of the frozen twenty miles of mother earth that stretch between Atchison and Leavenworth, let us turn to the latter city and glance at the preparations on foot for the proper reception of the anticipated guest.

The following announcement appeared in the Republican paper of Saturday, and was placarded about the streets:

The Hon. Abe Lincoln is on Kansas soil. He has spoken at Elwood, Troy, and Doniphan. Last night he spoke at Atchison. To-day, at noon, he arrives in Leavenworth; let us give the gallant champion of Freedom a reception befitting his great talents, his stirring eloquence, his noble-hearted devotion to the cause of Liberty.

*Chapter Four*

# Lincoln's Visit
# to Leavenworth

WITH THE PASSING of the Kansas-Nebraska Act in 1854, the lands in Kansas not designated as Indian Reservations were open for settlement. On the 9th of May that year, a group of men, the majority of whom were from Weston and Platte County, Missouri, met at Riveley's Store in Salt Creek Valley, about two miles west of Fort Leavenworth, to lay out the town of Leavenworth. The first public sale of lots was in October of that year and realized $12,600. Fort Leavenworth had been established in 1827 by Colonel Henry Leavenworth to protect pioneers from Indians as they moved west over the Oregon and Santa Fe Trails.

The city quickly grew, and by 1858 its population was shown by the 1859-1860 City Directory to be upwards of 10,000; it had become the largest city between St. Louis and San Francisco. The city was encouraged in its growth by the freighting firm of Russell, Majors, and Waddell, which had secured the military contract to haul supplies to distant Army posts. The firm hauled 16-million pounds of freight across the Oregon Trail during 1858 and 1859.

The 1858 Pike's Peak Gold Rush also increased the population of Leavenworth as people arrived by steamboats from the East to catch the stage for Denver. The Pike's Peak Express stagecoach left for its maiden run on July 2, 1859. It arrived in Denver a mere six days later. Passengers reported that ". . . the appointments of the route far exceeded our expectations. . . ."

By the time Abraham Lincoln arrived in Leavenworth in December 1859, the fire of 1858 had destroyed most of the original cottonwood frame buildings that made up the business section of the city. In just a few months, the eager inhabitants had replaced the burned buildings with more substantial and, in some cases, almost elegant brick buildings.

The steamboats on the Missouri River were the great highway of communication for travel and freight with the outside world. It was no uncommon sight to see four and five steamboats at the Leavenworth levee at one time, in those early days, loading and unloading freight of all kinds and passengers. Some boats were large enough to carry 400 passengers and 700 tons of freight. By the time Kansas was a territory, steamboats ran regular schedules and could be in St. Louis in about three days.

In 1857, the levee at Leavenworth was paved with cobblestones, giving the city the first steamboat landing west of St. Louis. It was just in time for the arrival of the Sisters of Charity — four sisters, two novices, and one orphan girl — on November 11, 1858. They came from Tennessee at the request of Bishop Miege, Vicar-Apostolic of Indian Territory, who was anxious to obtain a colony of sisters. They would open orphanages, start a hospital, an academy, junior college, and ultimately a four-year college — Saint Mary College.

After Horace Greeley attended the 1859 Osawatomie Convention, he visited Leavenworth for a second time. He judged that it had over 1,000 houses and was impressed by the city, but he was even more impressed by the Fort.

> The fort was a city of itself, with extensive barracks, capacious store-houses, several companies of soldiers, many fine

houses for officers, sutlers, etc., and a farm of twelve hundred acres. "It is a nice place, that Fort," he added, "with many excellent people about it; but I can't help asking what it costs, and who pays, and whether that little bill might not be somewhat docked without prejudice to the public interest. I believe it could."[1]

But Greeley opined that the greatest feature of Leavenworth was the Russell, Majors, and Waddell transportation establishment, located between the city and the fort:

Such acres of wagons! such pyramids of extra axletrees! such herds of oxen! such regiments of drivers and other employees! No one who does not see can realize how vast a business this is, or how immense are its outlays as well as its income. I presume this great firm has at this hour two millions of dollars invested in stock, mainly oxen, mules and wagons. (They last year employed six thousand teamsters, and worked forty-five thousand oxen.) Of course, they are capital fellows — so are those at the fort — but I protest against the doctrine that either army officers or army contractors, or both together, may have power to fasten slavery on a newly organized territory (as has just been done in New-Mexico) under the guise of letting the people of such territories govern themselves.[2]

As far as the surrounding land, the *Kansas State Gazetteer*, published in 1870, described it this way:

Leavenworth is situated in the midst of a beautiful section of country, with soil of surprising fertility, and in the summer one seems to be in the midst of a vast garden, skirted and interspersed with groves, hedges and cultivated fields; its prairies gemmed with countless flowers, all render its environs delightful, and combine to make it a beautiful spot.

Though Leavenworth's initial leanings were proslavery, having been formed by the proslavery men from Missouri, by 1859 it had become the home of a significant number of free-staters. The Republicans of

Leavenworth were a large enough group to give Abraham Lincoln a rousing welcome.

On the morning of Saturday, December 3rd, Lincoln was escorted from Atchison to Leavenworth where its citizens gave him a reception fitting for a future President. The event was reported by the *Leavenworth Daily Times* on December 5, 1859.

> Saturday was a wintry day. The sky was clear and a northern wind whistled over plain and street alike. But warm hearts and willing hands laughed the wintry elements to scorn. The coming of an honored man — crowned with Nature's patent of nobility — touched the hearts of our people and they paid him such loving tribute as to make the day seem one of sunshine, joy and peace. No conqueror, with trophies and hostages, circled by martial pomp, was he who came amongst us, and yet no laureled chief — with all the honors of bloody victories — was ever welcomed with more cordial cheer than honest Abe Lincoln by the Republicans of Leavenworth.
>
> It having previously announced that Hon. Abram Lincoln, of Illinois, was to visit Leavenworth at an early hour, preparations were made to give him a reception befitting the man, and the cause of which he is such an able and fearless champion. It was understood he would arrive on the outskirts of the city at 12 o'clock, and that the reception would take place at the Mansion House at 1 o'clock.
>
> A large number of citizens in carriages, on horseback and on foot, accompanied by the band, all under the direction of Capt. Dickson, the Marshal of the day, proceeded about a mile on the Government Lane, and there met our city's honored guest, greeting him with a rousing round of cheers — such as Republicans only can give.
>
> The procession then turned and proceeded to the city in the following order:
>
> 1. Band.
> 2. Citizens on foot.
> 3. Carriages.
> 4. Horseman.

Arriving at Turner's Hall the procession halted, and the large crowd then gave our guest three times three, while "the Kickapoo" was uttering a loud-mouthed welcome in thunder tones.

The procession then moved on through Delaware street, up Main and Shawnee to the Mansion House. There the crowd was so dense that it was difficult for the carriages to get through. Mr. Lincoln was received on the balcony of the Mansion by Col. J.C. Vaughan, who welcomes him in behalf of the Republicans of Leavenworth in a brief but appropriate speech.

Mr. Lincoln was called for with loud cheers and made a few remarks, alluding Briefly to political matters, giving a short sketch of the progress of the Republican party; of the trials of the Free State men in making this beautiful country the home of the free. He said their battles would never have to be fought over again. (Loud cries of "that's so," and "no! no!") and after returning his sincere thanks for so flattering a reception, and remarking that he should address them in the evening, he retired amid the cheers of the crowd.

Long before the time appointed for the speech, the Hall was filled to overflowing. — Many ladies were present. Mr. Lincoln was introduced to the audience by Col. Delahay, amid enthusiastic cheering. He spoke for about an hour and a half, and every few minutes were interrupted by the applause given.[3]

Lincoln began his speech:

"Ladies and Gentlemen: You are, as yet, the people of a Territory; but you probably soon will be the people of a State of the Union. Then you will be in possession of new privileges, and new duties will be upon you. You will have to bear a part in all that pertains to the administration of the National Government. That government, from the beginning, has had, has now, and must continue to have a policy in relation to domestic slavery . . . that policy must, of necessity, take one of two directions. It must deal with the institution as being wrong or as not being wrong. . . . Leave your Missouri neighbors alone . . . and so conduct yourselves that if you cannot be at peace with them, the fault shall be wholly theirs." Mr. Lincoln closed by an appeal to all — opponents as well as friends — to think soberly and maturely, and never fail to cast their vote, insisting that it was not a privilege only, but a duty to do so.[4]

The *Leavenworth Daily Times* report of December 5th continued:

We have not room to give even an outline of his speech. He showed up popular sovereignty in its true light; showed conclusively that the Democratic party of to-day was not the Democratic party of a few years ago; that the Democratic party was not a conservative party; that the Republican party was the only party in the Union that attempted to carry out the principles of Washington, Madison, Jefferson, and the founders of this Government.

After he concluded, many were eager to take by the hand one of whom they had heard so much.

Of the many receptions that Mr. Lincoln has received, we venture to assert that he never had a warmer one than that extended to him by the Republicans of Leavenworth on Saturday last.

The speech Lincoln gave in Leavenworth was, in essence, the same speech he would give two months later in New York. Looking at the main topics of these two speeches, one can see that they are the same. Both speeches included discussions of the intent of the "thirty-nine fathers" who signed the Constitution concerning slavery, the Republican position on slavery and the Democratic response to it, popular sovereignty, the Dred Scott decision, and John Brown.

Lincoln spoke for one and a half hours in Leavenworth, so he said much that is not in the published synopsis. He probably worked from rough outlines and tailored his speech somewhat to his audience — going more in depth in New England about the Constitution and saying more in Kansas about the popular sovereignty and the Kansas-Nebraska Act. However, it does seem likely that he worked from the same outline.

The fact that Lincoln edited the speech before it was published[5] in New

York is convincing that he had not prepared a word-for-word copy, or he would simply have given that to the papers. Rather, he edited copies that others had transcribed upon hearing his speech. A reporter for the *New York Daily Tribune* revisited the Leavenworth speech in an article published in August 1860. He outlined Lincoln's first speech and, while some of the terminology is different, Lincoln's general topics are the same as those listed above.[6]

Critics that claimed the New York speech propelled Lincoln toward the presidency largely overlooked the Leavenworth speech. Certainly any political event occurring in New York had a larger impact than one occurring in Kansas. A literary critic who was present at Lincoln's Cooper Institute speech reports how he was deeply moved by the speech — the same speech that had been given in Leavenworth:

> . . . when Lincoln arose to speak I was greatly disappointed in his appearance. He was tall, tall — oh, how tall! and so angular and awkward, that I had, for an instant, a feeling of pity for so ungainly a man. His clothes were black and ill-fitting, badly wrinkled — as if they had been jammed carelessly into a small trunk. His bushy head, with the stiff black hair thrown back, was balanced on a long and lean head-stalk, and when he raised his hands in an opening gesture, I noticed that they were very large. He began in a low tone of voice — as if he were used to speaking out-doors and was afraid of speaking too loud. He said "Mr. Cheerman" instead of "Mr. Chairman," and employed many other words with an old-fashioned pronunciation. I said to myself: "Old fellow, you won't do; its all very well for the wild West, but this will never do down in New York." But pretty soon he began to get into his subject; he straightened up, made regular and graceful gestures; his face lighted as with an inward fire; the whole man was transfigured. I forgot his clothes, his personal appearance, and his individual peculiarities. Presently, forgetting myself, I was on my feet with the rest, yelling like a wild Indian, cheering this wonderful man. In the close parts of his argument, you could hear the gentle sizzling of the gas-burners. When he reached a climax, the thunders of applause were terrific. It was a great speech.[7]

Abe Lincoln's ability to move people through the spoken word was similarly not wasted on the people of Leavenworth. They were so impressed that they asked him to speak again the same day at Stockton's Hall. In this speech, he clarified the Republican position on slavery, stating that there was no desire to interfere with slavery where it existed, but to prevent its extension to new territories. He also objected to his opponents' attempts to identify the Republican Party with the John Brown affair. John Brown had been hanged just three days prior in Virginia for the Harpers Ferry incident. Lincoln praised Brown for his great courage and rare unselfishness, but condemned his choice of violence and bloodshed as a way of solving the problem of slavery.

The *Leavenworth Daily Times*, on December 5, 1859, praised Lincoln's Saturday speech.

> The first characteristic of Mr. Lincoln is truthfulness. He has
> no clap trap in or about him. He is simple and downright. No

Stockton's Hall at 4th and Delaware Streets in Leavenworth in 1869.
*Kansas State Historical Society, Topeka*

# STOCKTON'S HALL,

## CORNER FOURTH AND DELAWARE STS.,

### LEAVENWORTH, KANSAS.

This new and magnificent Hall—the largest in the West—provided with

# EIGHT HUNDRED ARM CHAIRS,

A large and commodious Stage, with Exits and Entrances, being thoroughly heated, lighted and ventilated, and

### COMPLETE IN ALL OF ITS APPOINTMENTS,

#### MAY NOW BE OBTAINED FOR

## CONCERTS, LECTURES, DRAMATIC ENTERTAINMENTS,

## BALLS, PARTIES, &C.

### Address STOCKTON & CO., Lock Box No. 33,

### Leavenworth, Kansas.

Advertisement in the 1859-1860 *Leavenworth City Directory and Business Mirror.*

matter how he deals with parties, or the measures of parties, he deals with them plainly and justly. No speaker, in our belief, is freer from prejudice, or those passions which cloud intellect or narrow it. He seems what he believes to be truth and he presents it as he sees it. Men of heart and of truth, consequently, consider what he urges, whether they agree with him or not.

The second characteristic of Mr. Lincoln is, common sense. Oratory is an art. The mellow voice falls sweetly on the ear, and the rounded period dies away as a musical note. Yet there may be — often there is — no grit, no marrow, no food for reflection or thought — on the part of those thus gifted. It is all manner — passionate, persuasive, vehement — but it is the passion[,] the persuasion, the vehemence, generally of shallow feeling or animal impulse, and nothing more. Mr. Lincoln, on the contrary, [*is*] taking a broad common sense strength. He is clear and solid. His clearness and solidity, too, are felt, must be felt by bitterest opponents, save those among them who live upon the stimulus of party, or who seek to lead party.

Mr. Lincoln, consequently, is true to principle without being ultra. He plays no part, and he would have no political organization play a part, in State or national affairs. There is the Constitution of the Union. He stands by it and will do so while he lives. There is its great principle of freedom. He will compromise that for no triumph — yield it up for no defeat. Either the slaveholder has the right under the Constitution to bring his human chattels into the Territories of the Union, or he has not. If he has, we must submit. If he has not, we must restrain him. Hence he repudiates Squatter Sovereignty, and all and every clap trap which conceals or seeks to conceal the true issue, and he does it, too, with a force of logic which cannot be successfully resisted — with a power of reasoning which no mind or party can overthrow.

But better yet, Mr. Lincoln is full of hope and faith. The impatient sink down after defeat, and the impulsive grow weary after victory. He avoids both errors, and the people must avoid them, if they would defend their own rights or secure their own progress. It is the iron-will — it is the steady and oft repeated blow — it is the energy which never flags after victory or pales before defeat — which conquers. All history establishes this truth. All human experience proves it. Looking, then, to the progress of the cause of constitutional liberty, in the near past, and to the certainty of its success in the near future; Mr. Lincoln earnestly advocates the use of those means essential to win it. What is worth having, is worth working for. Let us be hopeful and active — let us have faith, and never tire whether defeat or victory crown our efforts. Mr. Lincoln's visit will do good to the Territory. No man can speak as he speaks or work as he works, without sowing seed which will bear rich fruit.

Not all local papers gave such a glowing report of Lincoln's speech. The *Leavenworth Weekly Herald*, a Democratic paper, of December 10, 1859, gave a very different view.

According to announcement this venerable champion of Republicanism arrived Saturday afternoon about 5 o'clock, and was immediately surrounded by a respectable crowd of the "faithful," who bore him to the Mansion House, where the ceremonies of introduction and reception were gone through with. Col. J.C. Vaughan introduced him to the crowd, when he responded in a short speech — the pith of which was "he could not speak long, as he was to address them at night." He was probably afraid he would explore his "one idea" and leave no capital for the evening.

## At Night

After elevating his nose, as if to scent the strength of the crowd in which he found himself, and taking a view all round, "Old Abe" took out his notes, squared himself like a man who had work before him and felt equal to the occasion.

The personal appearance of the individual is altogether different from any idea which a stranger would form. So far from appearing "old" he bears the appearance of a man well in his prime, but without dignity or grace; he has the lank, loose stamp of a six foot Egyptian "sucker," who has had his supply of whiskey cut off in his growing days, and therefore suddenly "ran to seed." His style of delivery, though concise, and striking plainly on the hearer, bears the impress of labored efforts to collect a smooth and easy flow; while his ideas are put forth in language totally at variance with all rules of grammar.

We cannot review it in all its particulars; but we have seldom heard one where more spurious argument, cunning sophistry, and flimsy evasions, were mingled together, and made to work out all right — no doubt to the satisfaction of his audience. He seized the slavery hobby in the beginning and rode it out to the end; starting out with presumed facts, which the man could not but know were points in dispute in the war of parties, and by the surreptitious adoption of which he cunningly evaded any charge of inconsistency in his erratic and blundering harangue. His remarks throughout were but the reproduction of the same old Illinois stump speeches with which he bored his audiences in that campaign which made him famous, and gave him the notoriety which he is not entitled to, owing to the position of his opponent. He certainly has the same old arguments stereotyped, which, if reports be true, he treats his audiences to on each and every occasion. The most noticeable point was his appeal to the Republican in Kansas, "to let the slaves in Missouri alone; no doubt he thought they needed some advice on this subject. His last remarks were confined to a vindication of the policy and doctrines of modern republicanism, and here is where the weakness of the man was apparent. His reply to the charge of sectionalism was flimsy, and weak in the extreme, accompanied with the hesitating delivery and excruciating gesture of a man who finds himself upon ground with which he is unaquainted, and accordingly "old Abe" beat a hasty retreat, and wound up with the apology that "as he had to speak again on Monday, he could not say more"; afraid of taxing that one idea too heavily.

Quantum sufficit. "Honest Abraham" will not make one more Republican voter in this Territory. Bring on another importation of "blooded stock," gentlemen.[8]

The Republicans of Lawrence wanted Lincoln to visit their city and handed him a letter of invitation on Saturday, December 3rd. It was written by L. L. Jones, a young free-stater lawyer, who came from Connecticut, and signed by 13 other Lawrence Republicans.

*Lawrence Nov 29th 1859*

*Dear A. Lincoln!*

*Dear Sir!*

*You __may perhaps__ recollect me, as formerly resident in Chicago, and as __somewhat__ identified with the good Republicans of that goodly Republican City, in the famous fight, they made with you, and __for you__, last year — I came to Kansas last summer, and am settled here, practicing law __and__ Republicanism —*

My object in addressing you, is to invite you, and earnestly solicit you, to visit our City and to speak here.

This I do in behalf of the many Republicans here, to whom the mention of your name is as a "house-hold word."

You live in their minds and hearts, and your coming will kindle a stronger enthusiasm for our Party and Principles — if that be possible — than has ever heretofor burned here, in this the centre and the core of Free Principles in our territory —

If your time and engagements in Kansas will permit — you _must_ visit us — If you _can come_, please advise me, of the day you will be with us.

Yours very truly

L L Jones

We cordially concur in the above invitation and request.

E. S. Lowman      S. O. Thacher
S. B. Prentiss      S. C. Smith
Lyman Allen      James C. Horton
O. G. Bassitt      E. M. Deitzler
L. W. Eldridge      Caleb Pratt
C. W. Batavek      George W. Smith
H. Shanklin⁹

After Lincoln returned home, he wrote to Mr. Jones from Springfield:

L.L. Jones, Esq        Springfield, Ills.

My dear Sir:        Dec. 9, 1859

Your kind invitation to me to visit Lawrence, was handed me at Leavenworth on Saturday the 3rd. Inst. I was advertised to speak there that evening and also on Monday the 5th; so that it *was not possible for me to be at Lawrence before, or at, the election. I supposed there was not sufficient object for me to go after the election, through the excessive cold.*

*Please present my respects, and make my acknowledgments, to the other gentlemen, who joined you in the invitation, and accept the same for yourself. Very truly yours     A Lincoln*[10]

The resident reporter for the *New York Daily Tribune* reported on Lincoln's activities the day after his Leavenworth speech, Sunday, December 4th. Lincoln was staying at the Delahays' home.

On the ensuing Sabbath Mr. Lincoln confined himself to the house in company and association with a few particular friends. Monday morning found him on the alert. He took equal pleasure in renewing old acquaintances or forming new ones. He was to be found on the street, in offices or workshops, and took especial delight in familiarizing himself with our people, their pursuits and convictions. In the afternoon he delivered another speech to an immense audience.[11]

On December 6, 1859, the *Leavenworth Daily Times* covered Lincoln's second speech.

## SECOND SPEECH OF HON. ABE LINCOLN.

### STOCKTON'S HALL A JAM.

Eloquent effort and great enthusiasm.

Pursuant to notice, Hon. Abe Lincoln addressed the citizens of Leavenworth, yesterday, at Stockton's Hall. The day was fearfully unpleasant, but the Hall was filled to overflowing — even ladies being present.

Mr. Lincoln opened by reviewing the Territorial policy of our Government at the start, proving conclusively that it was in favor of liberty and was ever so exerted except in some of the Southern States where slavery existed by municipal law or was made a distinctive feature of the articles of cession. But where these causes were not here was freedom proclaimed.

The Fathers did not seek to interfere with slavery where it existed but to prevent its extension. This was the policy of the Republican party of to-day.

The divisions of sentiment in the Democratic party in regard to slavery were flimsy and immaterial. The most advanced element could boast of no higher sentiment than an indifference to the peculiar institution. No part of the Democracy ever declared slavery wrong in itself; and they reached a sublime height when they said they didn't care whether it was voted up or voted down.

This indifference was all the slave-power could ask. It was a virtual recognition of the right of slavery to universal extension.

If a house was on fire there could be but two parties. One in favor of putting out the fire. Another in favor of the house burning. But these popular sovereignty fellows would stand aloof and argue against interfering. — The house must take care of itself subject only to the constitution and the conditions of fire and wood.

The speaker alluded, with much force and wit, to the great line (which we are assured by Senator Douglas was ordained of God) on one side of which slave-labor alone could be employed — on the other free-labor. Thought the Missouri River might be the line referred to. If the line was ordained of God it ought to be plain and palpable, but he had never been able to put his finger upon it.

The attempt to identify the Republican party with the John Brown business was an electioneering dodge. Was glad to know that the Democracy underrated the good sense of the people as the great Republican victories in New York, New Jersey, Minnesota and Iowa — where the argument was brought out with extraordinary emphasis — clearly demonstrated. In Brown's hatred of slavery the speaker sympathized with him. But Brown's insurrectionary attempt he emphatically denounced. He believed the old man insane, and had yet to find the first Republican who endorsed the proposed insurrection. If there was one he would advise him to step out of the ranks and correct his politics. But slavery was responsible for their uprisings. They were fostered by the institution. In 1830-31, the slaves themselves arose and killed fifty-eight whites in a single night. These servile upheavings must be continually occurring where slavery exists.

The democracy was constituted of two great elements. First. The original and unadulterated Democrats. Second. The Old line and *eminently* conservative Whigs. This incongruous party was ever charging the Republicans with favoring negro suffrage, sustaining this charge by instancing the two Republican States of Massachusetts and New Hampshire where negroes are allowed to vote. But it so happens that the law conferring this franchise was enacted by the Old Whigs in Massachusetts and the Democrats in New Hampshire. Kansas was the only State where the Republicans had the framing of the organic law and here they they [*sic*] confined the elective franchise to the white man alone.

Mr. Lincoln said that, *in political arguments*, the Democracy turned up their noses at "amalgamation." But while there were only one hundred and seventy-nine mulattoes in the Republican State of New Hampshire, there were *seventy-nine thousand* in the good old Democratic State of Virginia — and the only notable instance of amalgamation that occurred to him was in the case of a Democratic Vice President.

Mr. Lincoln wanted the races kept distinct. Because he did not wish to hold a negro woman as a slave it did not follow that he wanted her for a wife. Such flimsy diatribes were perpetrated by the Democracy to divert the public mind from the real issue — the extension or the non-extension of slavery — its localization or nationalization.

Mr. Lincoln closed by a clear and forcible definition of the aims and the principles of the Republican party. He showed how they harmonized with the teachings of those by whom the Government was founded and how their predominance was essential to the proper development of our country — its progress and its glory — to the salvation of the Union and the perpetuity of Free Institutions.

We have given but the merest outline of Mr. Lincoln's

speech, which we count among his ablest and happiest efforts. He sought to make no display, but gave home-bred truths in a home-bred style that touched the hearts of his hearers and went home to all. The noble sentiments he uttered and the force of his logic carried conviction with them and aroused an earnest enthusiasm. At the close of his speech he was greeted with cordial round of cheers which made the old hall ring.

Once again the *Leavenworth Weekly Herald* did not agree:

Abram Lincoln Again. — This last importation of the Blacks again addressed a shivering squad of his admirers at Stockton's Hall yesterday.

An effort was made beforehand to persuade him to touch more directly upon our political history, and serve up "bleeding Kansas" in his peculiar and forcible style, but he preferred to stick to his "nigger," and twang upon the old and worn out arguments, which by some inexplicable operation have been stereotyped upon his brain.

Again he seized upon the subject of slavery at the outset, and after borrowing largely from his harangue on Saturday evening, went into a long strain of vilification, invective and abuse against all who opposed him and his party. His audience cheered and clapped him on, in his miserable attempt to make capital out of the occasion, by prostituting his ability to pander to an animosity which delights itself in slurring personalities, and filthy expectorations against the opposition.

It is a wonder to many how such a man as Abram Lincoln, can so prostitute himself. Is there no other issue in this wide country, but that of "nigger"? Has he forever and firmly wedded his talents and ability in the fanatical crusade of Abolitionism, and sees nothing upon the political horizons but the African? Where, we ask, are those issues, which he once battled with a worthiness which won him renown? Are they dead? No, but he has forgotten their importance, and has allowed himself to be irrevocably drawn into the whirlpool of fanaticism.

He had a word to say of Old John Brown. (Cheers for Brown.) So far as Brown's sentiments for the negro were

concerned, he sympathized with him; (cheers) but he condemned his lawlessness and bloodshed; (a faint cheer;) and he
had yet to hear the first Republican say, he supported him in it.
(Old Abe paused in expectation of applause, but it didn't come;
his hearers were not with him there.)

In reply to this balderdash, we would ask him if Conway,
Thatcher, Lane & Co., of this Territory, are not Republicans?
and if they did not support Brown, why did they hold sympathy
meetings at Lawrence, on the day of his execution? Why did the
prominent Republican leaders in the States do the same thing,
and raise money for him and his? "Honest Abram" don't read
the papers, or if he does, he's blinded by the "negro."

His whole speech was but just such trumpery as the above,
and every position had about as much foundation. We don't
wonder that Douglas rakes the man "fore and aft," for he is
"open" enough, and shows a good target between "wind and
water." To sum up the whole, we characterize his efforts as
weak in the extreme and himself an imbecile old fogy of one
idea; and that is — nigger, nigger, nigger.[12]

These two very different newspaper accounts of Lincoln's visit to Leavenworth are representative of the papers of the day. As author Cecil Howes
noted, ". . . editors were proud to take sides on any questions of moment.
. . . There was no sitting on the fence in those days. You were either for or
against slavery. . . ."[13] and you acted accordingly. Their words were direct
and they said what they meant. The following article describing Colonel
Daniel Anthony is an example of the direct language newspapers used in
those early days:

The fiendish, bloodthirsty proprietor of the Leavenworth
Times, is so fearfully low down and utterly despicable, here,
where he is thoroughly known, that the very dogs, the sorriest
mongrels or the mangiest Spitz, would, in a certain contin-
gency, pass him by, and cross a county writhing with agony, in
search of a cleaner post. For twenty-two years, it has been his
habit to call decent men, who opposed his lunacies, "dirty
dogs," "gamblers," "skunks," "drunkards," "scoundrels" etc.
His beastiality of disposition, and brutishness of heart, have

banished him from the walk in life of every gentleman, and he stalks through our streets, despised, shunned, and hideous to the sight of those who, with gentle instincts or cultivated habits, loathe disagreeable or disgusting surroundings.

Ignoring decency, to answer an argument, or refute a charge, he ever resorts to his vocabulary of billingsgate which springs spontaneous from a putrid heart, and scatters his blackguardism in very poor English. Gentlemen, congregated on the sidewalk, scatter at his approach, as though a cyclone of epidemic pestilence was imminent, and ladies shudder, as they drop their veils and shrink with horror, when they realize his vicinage. . . ."[14]

Newspapermen, especially editors, never backed away from verbal, and in many cases physical, fights. According to Howe,

During territorial days and through much of the Civil War period every Kansas editor also packed a gun. The old Colt's horse pistol was as much the necessary equipment of an editor in those days as was his pencil and a piece of scratch paper. . . .[15]

Daniel R. Anthony of Leavenworth was one of the early "pistol-packing pencil pushers." Anthony came to Kansas with Charles Robinson and the first Emigrant Aid Company, then started a newspaper in Leavenworth. His Quaker father had been disciplined by the Church for marrying out of the meeting and buttoning his coat contrary to meeting rules. Finally, he was expelled for permitting his children to dance at home. His children, son Daniel and daughter, Susan B. Anthony — the suffragette — reflected their father's independent streak.[16]

Daniel's lifestyle evidenced his rebellious nature. As a newspaper editor, he carried two big horse pistols and, during the course of his life, fought a duel, was shot at numerous times, was seriously wounded once, and killed a rival editor. In 1859, Anthony and Daniel W. Wilder published *The Conservative*, a Republican newspaper. Later Anthony would purchase the *Leavenworth Times*. The rival newspaper was the *Leavenworth Herald*, a Democratic paper, and the editor was R. C. Satterlee. After a verbal war through their papers, Satterlee and Anthony met one day in the street and exchanged more heated words, followed by an exchange of bullets. Satterlee was killed and Anthony's companion was wounded.[17] Daniel Anthony was acquitted of the murder, but this would not be the end of his shoot-outs with other editors. In 1875, Anthony was shot by W. W. Embry of the *Leavenworth Appeal*. His sister, Susan B. Anthony came to nurse him. For over a month she took turns with others holding a finger on the artery over Anthony's collarbone to control the flow of blood. During his convalescence, Anthony became irritated by the Salvation Army Band playing in front of his building and proceeded to kick his foot through the bass drum, leaving his boot stuck in the drumhead.[18]

Daniel R. Anthony, editor of the *Leavenworth Times*.
*Kansas State Historical Society, Topeka*

Daniel Anthony's strong personality was evident later when, as a Lieutenant Colonel, he served as second in command to Colonel Charles R. Jennison and the Kansas Seventh during the Civil War. His violent temper, harsh tongue, and overbearing manner kept him from being liked by his men and insured that he would come into conflict with the equally strong personality of Jennison. Anthony was very serious about his duties with the Army, and when Jennison was advanced to Brigade Commander, Anthony was placed in charge of the Seventh. For all of his shortcomings, Anthony was a hard-working leader and, unlike Jennison, insisted that the Seventh become a well-drilled and strictly disciplined organization. He also tried to move the unit away from its "Jayhawking habits" that had been allowed by Jennison.[19] Anthony's actions clearly did not please his men and desertions became a problem. He was ultimately able to regain his men's respect when he refused to return freed slaves to their masters, as ordered by his superiors, so as to not violate the Fugitive Slave Law. Anthony was arrested for refusing to obey orders and eventually his resignation from the military was accepted.

After the war, Jennison and Anthony continued to oppose each other in local politics and disagreed on other issues that led to a final climactic shoot-out on May 13, 1865. Though there was a question as to who shot first, both fired their weapons. Anthony's shot struck Jennison in the leg and Jennison's shot missed. Jennison was brought to trial but was acquitted.[20]

Daniel Anthony was twice elected mayor of Leavenworth and continued to be a powerful man in the politics of Kansas. Asked in 1904, on his deathbed, what he would change if he could live is life again, he replied, "Next time I'd be more positive."[21]

Daniel Anthony was in Leavenworth when Lincoln visited and told the following story in a *Kansas City Star* interview in 1902.

Most of the free-state men of influence in the town were from New York or New England, aside from the Germans, and favored Senator Seward, of New York, for the presidency. Lincoln was out of Congress, had been defeated for the senate, and his candidacy for the republican nomination did not impress the young Easterners. Mrs. Delahay, wife of the judge, was a kins-woman of Lincoln — a cousin, I believe — and the Illinois ex-congressman was coming to Leavenworth to visit her. We had notice of his coming, and the Wilders, both of them, I think, John Hatterscheidt, William Tholen and I drove in a carriage to Doniphan, a few miles north of Atchison, to meet him. We found him at the tavern, where a committee from Troy had brought him, and we drove back to Leavenworth. He took a room at the Planters', and went from there to the Delahays. That night he made a free-state speech, and we gave him as good a reception as if Seward had never been heard of.

After the meeting he came to a room occupied by Carter Wilder, Tholen and me. It was across the street from the hotel, on the second floor, and contained two beds, a cot, some plain chairs, and an old box stove. That stove could eat wood enough to keep one man busy carrying fuel up the stairs and two or three men poor paying for it. Lincoln and Marcus J. Parrott, the Kansas delegate in Congress, were our guests, and they stayed until all the wood in the room had been devoured by the glutton stove.

It was a cold night, as I remember it, and nobody was willing to leave the room long enough to go for wood. Mark Parrott had sent us great sacks full of patent-office reports from Washington to distribute among the boys. Times were not dull enough in the town to make government reports popular reading-matter, and many sacks full of bound paper were unopened in the room. Some had already served for fuel, and when the fire died down two or three bulky books went into the stove.

We were all Seward men, and Mr. Lincoln knew it. Up to this time, out of courtesy to our guest, no one had mentioned politics; for, while Lincoln was ostensibly visiting his kins-woman, Mrs. Delahay, it was well known that he wasn't forgetting the national convention of the next year. Besides, Delahay was his Kansas champion. Lincoln afterward appointed him United States judge. As the books were heaved into the stove one of the men asked: "Mr. Lincoln, when you become president will you sanction the burning of government reports by cold men in Kansas territory?" "Not only will I not sanction it, but I will cause legal action to be brought against the offenders," said Lincoln, smiling good-naturedly. That's the only reference to the presidency made that night, and every man in the room was a politician. Lincoln sat there for hours, his feet against the stove, and his chair tilted back. His reputation as a storyteller is deserved, for he was the leader in swapping tales that night. None of them, however, was sufficiently funny, strong or unique to make a forty-years impression on me. I can't recall a single one of them. It was simply a winter evening of talk among young men who liked to talk. There was nothing to drink, but some of the men were smoking.

In appearance Lincoln was not the impressive man the next

few years made him. He was made up of head, hands, feet, and length. The lines that gave his face and figure a majesty of sadness were yet to come.[22]

Lincoln stayed over for the Tuesday election on December 6, 1859, in which state officers and a representative to Congress were chosen under the new Wyandotte Constitution.[23] Leavenworth was the stronghold of Democratic strength in the Territory. In spite of Mark Delahay's confidence that Lincoln's visit to Kansas would have a dramatic effect on the election, the results were mostly Democratic wins. In the December 6th election, Leavenworth County cast 1,404 votes for Samuel Medary — the Democratic candidate for Governor — and 997 votes for Charles L. Robinson — the Republican candidate. Perhaps the impact of Abe Lincoln's visit was greater in Doniphan and Atchison Counties, as they both voted a majority for the Republicans. As far as Delahay's promise to deliver Kansas for Lincoln if he would come and try out his Presidential campaign speech, the six Kansas delegates all voted for Seward one month later in Chicago. Lincoln never got a vote from Kansas.[24]

The *Leavenworth Daily Times* on December 6, 1859, spoke of Lincoln's departure.

This gentleman leaves us this morning for the East. His short stay in Kansas has been full of significance. He has met a reception that would be accorded to but few in the nation, and he has sown seed that cannot but be productive of great good. We part with him regretfully and we echo but the sentiments of our people when we wish for him a long life and the honors befitting such a gallant captain in the army of Freedom.

Abe Lincoln came to us no stranger but his presence and his words have drawn him closer to our hearts. He is our friend — the friend of Kansas — and he will ever find the latch-string out when he may choose to honor us with another visit. Full of gratitude for services rendered, of admiration for his heroic qualities we bid honest Abe a kind and heart-felt farewell.

Although there has been some debate as to Lincoln's transportation on his return trip — some believed he returned to St. Joseph, Missouri, by steamboat — the *Leavenworth Daily Times* reported on December 7th, the day that Lincoln left, that "The River opposite this city has been frozen over since Sunday morning. The ice on an average is six inches thick, and many persons and horses crossed with safety yesterday." W. H. Gill, the editor of the *Leavenworth Weekly Herald*, the Democratic paper, on December 10th, printed a wonderful account of Lincoln's return trip to St. Joseph.

At 9 o'clock this morning, wrapped up as comfortably as shawls, blankets, over coats, and Buffalo robes could make me, I took passage in open wagon, for this city [*St. Joseph*], where I had the pleasure of arriving, at 4 o'clock, without a broken bone.

I can't say the trip was unpleasant, although our wagon was destitute of either cover or springs. The weather was cool enough for all practicable purposes but nothing like so piercing as for some days previous. My fellow-passengers were the Hon.A. Lincoln, of Ill, Hon. M.J. Parrott, (on his way to the Federal Capitol), Mr. Lawrence, the clever and gentlemanly agent of the H. & Mo. R.R. [*Hannibal and St. Joseph Railroad*] and Mr. Hughes, of the Palmyra Courier, who informs me that he has made some handsome investments in our city, believing it to be the point north of St. Louis.

Judge Lincoln was the soul of the company. Whilst we abhor the political heresies to which he adheres, none can deny that he is a high-toned, honorable and dignified gentleman. He has an inexhaustible store of the humorous in his composition, although his appearance would indicate that he was the gravest of the grave. His numerous anecdotes, most happily related, produced many a hearty laugh from his companions, and did much to relieve the monotony of our otherwise rough and tedious trip.

The "Judge," and he declines the title, as he says he has never filled a Judicial position, is wonderfully in love with Kansas, or what he has seen of it. For beauty and sublimity he pronounces it superior to any country he has ever beheld. Of Leavenworth, he gives the same opinion expressed by all men of taste and judgment who have seen it — that its site is unsurpassed in beauty, its growth without a parallel, and that no jealous rivals or petty misrepresentations can prevent its attaining a proud position among the great cities of our country.

On political matters, the Judge inclined to be somewhat "offish." Perhaps the fact the Democratic majority in our city, has been recently largely increased, even after his two able speeches, had a tendency to disgust him with politics. We sought to relieve him on this point, however, by assuring him that he had instilled all the spirit and enthusiasm in his party that had been manifested, and that the Democratic majority would have been five hundred instead of three, had he not aroused his sluggish, slumbering Abolition brethren.

Lincoln spent the evening of Wednesday, December 7th, in St. Joseph, and at five o'clock Thursday morning he again took the Hannibal and St. Joseph Railroad home. Lincoln confirmed his reported impression of Leavenworth in a letter he wrote to a friend who asked his advice as to where to begin his career. Lincoln wrote:

> *If I went West, I think I would go to Kansas — to Leavenworth or Atchison. Both these are and will continue to be, fine growing places.*[25]

An article from the *Springfield State Journal* confirms Lincoln's pleasure with his trip to Kansas:

> Mr. Lincoln returned home from his recent visit to Kansas night before last. He expresses himself delighted with his visit and with the cordial reception he met with from the people of that incipient state. During his visit Mr. Lincoln made six speeches, one at Elwood, one at Troy, and one at Doniphan, all in Doniphan county; one at Atchison, in Atchison county, and two in Leavenworth city. At all he had very large and enthusiastic audiences. The election occurred on the 5th and the returns thus far indicate that the republicans did their whole duty, having made great gains on the vote of the former election.[26]

The reporter for the *New York Daily Tribune* might have summed up Lincoln's visit to Leavenworth best:

I have purposely reserved an account of Mr. Lincoln's reception and stay at Leavenworth — the metropolis of Kansas — both because it accords with the "march of events," and is deserving of enlarged mention. There was in it a peculiar significance. Though we have received many distinguished guests, we have had nothing that approximated to that ovation. It came so naturally — was so spontaneous and heartfelt — the enthusiasm over him and about him was so earnest — the regard for him so universal and penetrating, that we had rather to restrain than excite. The people recognized in him an honest man — one who had fought a good fight, and who was in it and for it for life. What wonder then that Mr. Lincoln regards his visit to Leavenworth as one of the happiest events in his life, or that the recollection of that event is, to us, a memory and a joy forever?

There are but few statesmen who could have been forced to do the work in which Abraham Lincoln <u>volunteered</u>. In dead of Winter he left the comforts of an attractive home to couple his energies with those of a young people in a distant Territory battling for the RIGHT. And when the petty maligners of our men and principles charge a mercenary spirit upon Abraham Lincoln, tell them for Kansas, that, though we pressed upon him such moneyed recompense as our poor means would admit, for services and sacrifices that no money could repay, he firmly declined all remuneration, and told us our satisfaction was more than a sufficient return for the little he had done. In justice both to our people and to Mr. Lincoln, it must be said that during the latter's visit no one ever dreamed he would occupy his present exalted position. We loved and honored <u>the man</u> in his plain and simple dignity of character. He stood before us as an illustration of what industry, integrity, and principle will accomplish. In no instance did he allude to himself in connection with any office or position. Frankly he spoke of the most conspicuous candidates for the Republican nomination, to all of whom he rendered a discriminating need of praise. He predicted the disruption of the Democracy and the certainty of our success in 1860, and he looked hopefully forward to a better day for our great Republic. His cordial reception in Kansas only evidenced the strong hold he had upon the popular heart, and may be regarded, in view of subsequent events, as a significant indication of a sentiment wide as our nation, deep as the human heart — a sentiment and impulse which rose and strengthened like a mighty billow, till it pointed to him — to Honest Abe — as the Man for the hour and the Crisis.[27]

## Chapter Five

# Lincoln: Memoirs and Stories

ONE OF THE first-hand reports we have of Abraham Lincoln's visit to Leavenworth is from the memoirs of Mary Delahay, the 15-year-old daughter of Mark Delahay. Mary, who was called Mollie, was one of five children — Julia, Edward, Robert, and Charles. Both the Lincolns and the Delahays had sons named Edward Baker after Mark Delahay's law partner in Illinois, Colonel Edward D. Baker, who was also a friend of Lincoln. (Lincoln's son, Eddie, had died of tuberculosis in 1850 when he was four years old.) After the first night at the Planters Hotel, Lincoln stayed with the Delahays, quickly making friends with the Delahay children. Mary shared her memories of Lincoln in the evenings at their home.

In personal appearance, Mr. Lincoln was not at all prepossessing. But he was very magnetic. He was so tall he had to stoop as he went up the stairway that led to our guest room. He was always informal and when nobody but the family was present he would always remove his shoes after supper as we sat about the fire in the back parlor. He asked my father to lend him some slippers, laughing heartily, and said: "I clean forgot to bring my slippers." He enjoyed the joke of having feet too large for any shoes about the place. Removing his shoes was a signal to us children that stories were forthcoming. We would gather about him, my sister Julia (later wife of Thomas Osborne, Governor of Kansas in 1872-6 and minister to Chile and then Brazil), my brothers, Edward Baker, Robert, Charles and I, to listen to fascinating stories. Mr. Lincoln preferred to sit in a low rosewood rocker which was not at all correct for his great length of six feet and four inches. But he always settled in that chair and before he had removed the second shoe we were around him. Such homely shoes he wore, and such long-footed gray wool socks with white heel and toe.

I remember one night Mother allowed us to stay up past bed time as the story telling was too absorbing to come to an untimely close. Mr. Lincoln interspersed references to his boys with the action of the story, and making it seem so real he would laugh: "Shall I give them to you girls? Mary, there is Robert for you, and Julia, you may have Willie, But what about Tad? What shall I do about him — there is no girl for him" Then he chuckled and repeated what Tad said when people asked him his name: "My name is Tod, but they call me Tommie Tad tometime." And Mr. Lincoln's great voice would roar in laughter.[1]

Mary told a wonderful story about Lincoln's boots that had occurred during the Republican convention. Lincoln wore size 14 congress gaiters and at the end of an arduous day, he returned to the hotel room and removed one of his boots, remarking to his son that he felt like there was something in the toe of his shoe. His son tapped the heel of the shoe on the floor and shook out of it a full-grown mouse, much to the amusement of all present.[2]

Mary Delahay — age 86
on February 1, 1930.
*Kansas State Historical*
*Society, Topeka*

Mary thought his socks strange, but the Delahay children were fortu-
nate, as Lincoln was known to wear his boots with no socks, or, much to
his wife Mary Todd Lincoln's chagrin, to wrap his feet in paper rather than
wear the socks she so carefully knitted him. Mary recalled that one day
during Lincoln's visit, her mother was worried because Robert would not
eat the proper amount of food.

> Mr. Lincoln turned with the kindliest smile as Mother protested
> with her small son that he must eat food or he would not grow,
> and said: "Don't worry, boys eat if they get good and hungry."[3]

Lincoln's visit was a great occasion for the Delahay family. Mary's mother, Louisiana, honored their guest by using, at every meal, the French china with gold bandings, and silver and crystal, usually reserved for state occasions. The children, bedecked in their Sunday best, even new shoes, were allowed to partake of the company supper every night.

Louisiana Delahay kept a Minton Jug in a place of honor on the parlor mantel. Being a utilitarian at heart and probably with no concept of the value of the pitcher, Lincoln took the china pitcher and went outside to the pump to get a fresh drink of water. Mary was, as she said, "petrified," when she saw Lincoln swing the fragile treasure against the iron mouth of the pump, chipping the lip of the pitcher. Lincoln, unaware of the accident, strode back into the house and graciously offered refreshment. Mary watched her mother's smiling countenance as she glanced at the broken pitcher, but her expression did not change; Mrs. Delahay was the perfect hostess.[4]

Louisiana Hanks Delahay.     *Richard A. Hanks Collection*

There is another pitcher story having to do with Abe Lincoln's visit to Leavenworth, this one concerning a white earthenware Wedgwood pitcher, decorated with hanging vines and clusters of grapes. According to the story, Lincoln had heard that a Leavenworth brewery made some of the best beer in the area and he wanted to taste it. The beer was brought, and

Abraham Lincoln drank beer from this Wedgwood pitcher in 1859, at the home of Mark Delahay.

Mary Delahay poured the beer for Lincoln and saw him drink it. She later gave the pitcher to the Leavenworth Chapter of the Daughters of the American Revolution with a notation written on the bottom: "From this pitcher Mr. A. Lincoln drank a glass of beer when a guest of my father, Mark W. Delahay, in 1859, at Leavenworth, Kansas, Kiowa St., near 3d St., M.E.D." August Uebline, the Leavenworth brewer, after hearing Lincoln's impressive speech, later claimed that "It was my good beer that inspired Lincoln and helped him withstand the cold."[5] The pitcher is now in the collection of the Frontier Army Museum at Fort Leavenworth, Kansas.

Mary, a typical 15-year-old, was eager to ask Lincoln to write in her new autograph album that had red covers traced in gold. When she shyly asked him,

> He smiled, held out his hand to take the little book and said, "This is the first time I have ever been so honored. I do not know what to write," But as he talked his hand began to move and his pen fly across the white page of my album. This is what he wrote:

> *Dear Mary: It is with pleasure I write my name in your album. Ere long some younger man will be happy to bestow his*

A rare photograph of William
"Buffalo Bill" Cody.
*Kansas State Historical Society, Topeka*

*name upon you. Don't allow it, Mary, until you are fully
assured that he is worthy of the happiness. Your Friend,
A. Lincoln.*

A good friend of Mary's was Julia Cody, the older sister of William
"Buffalo Bill" Cody — probably the most famous person raised in Leav-
enworth. The Codys lived about eight miles north of town. On the day that
Lincoln was in town, Julia Cody rode her horse into Leavenworth to get
the mail and, of course, she stopped to visit her friend Mollie Delahay.
Julia takes up the story from there:

> Mollie came out to meet me and to take me into the House.
> She and her mother both sayed, "Oh Julia, we are so glad you

came in today, for we are going to have Mr. Lincoln here for dinner." Julia said "Oh, I can't stay for dinner in this costume, for I had just put my riding habit over a gingham Dress. Mrs. Delahay sayed to Mollie, You run acrost and get Julia one of Maria's Dresses, as Maria and I were the same size, and Mollie was tall and thin; I was short and stout, but Mollie got a pretty white Dress for me, and I stayed and Eate dinnr with Abraham Lincoln, which I have always been proud to tell. I was late getting home, and Mother was beginning to worry about what was keeping me, but when I told her she was so glad, for she sayed he was to be our next President, and as we all thought he was, and I was so glad I got to see him and to tell I had Dined with; and that was 1860.[7] [*Julia was confused about the year; it was 1859.*]

The Codys shared the antislavery view of the Delahays. Isaac Cody, Julia and William's father, was stabbed while making a Free-State speech on September 18, 1854. It was a wound that, his family believed, contributed to his death on March 10, 1857.

Buffalo Bill, in his memoirs, related the incident:

In this war of vengeance the Cody family did not escape a full measure of affliction. Near the Salt Creek trading post was another store, kept by a Missourian named Rively, around which a considerable settlement had been made, which became the rendezvous of many different elements, and particularly of proslavery men, who enjoyed Rively's sympathies. In the summer of 1854, and within a few months after the "Enabling Act" was passed, a very large meeting was held at the popular rendezvous, and father being present was pressed to address the crowd on the slavery question, he being regarded as favorable disposed to making Kansas a slave territory, owing to the fact that his brother, Elijah, was a Missourian.

After much urging he at length spoke substantially as follows:

"GENTLEMEN: You have called upon me for a speech, and I have accepted your invitation rather against my will, as my views may not accord with the sentiments of a majority of this assembly. My remarks will therefore be brief and to the point. The question before us to-day is, shall the territory of Kansas admit slavery, and hereafter, upon her admission, shall she be a slave State? The question of slavery is itself a broad one, which will not permit of discussion at length in this place. I apprehend that your motive in calling upon me is to have me express my sentiments in regard to the introduction of slavery into Kansas. I shall gratify your wishes in that respect. I was one of the pioneers of the State of Iowa, and aided in its settlement when it was a territory, and helped to organize it as a State.

"Gentlemen, I voted that it should be a white state — that negroes, whether free or slave, should never be allowed to locate within its limits; and, gentlemen, I say to you now, and I say it boldly, that I propose to exert all my power in making Kansas the same kind of a State as Iowa. I believe in letting slavery remain as it now exists, and I shall always oppose its further extension. These are my sentiments, gentlemen, and let me tell you —"

He never finished this sentence, or his speech, His expressions were anything but acceptable to the rough-looking crowd, whose ire had been gradually rising to fever heat, and at this point they hooted and hissed him, and shouted, "You black Abolitionist, shut up!" "Get down from that box!" "Kill him!" "Shoot him!" and so on. Father, however, maintained his position on the dry goods box, notwithstanding the excitement and numerous invitations to step down, until a hot-headed pro-slavery, who was in the employ of my Uncle Elijah, crowded up and said: "Get off that box, you black Abolitionist, or I'll pull you off."

Father paid but little attention to him, and attempted to resume his speech, intending doubtless to explain his position and endeavor to somewhat pacify the angry crowd. But the fellow jumped up on the box, and pulling out a huge bowie knife, stabbed father twice, who reeled and fell to the ground. The man sprang after him, and would have ended his life then and there, had not some of the better men in the crowd interfered in time to prevent him from carrying out his murderous intention.

The excitement was intense, and another assault would probably have been made on my father, had not Rively hurriedly carried him to his home. There was no doctor within any reasonable distance, and father at once requested that he be conveyed in the carriage to his brother Elijah's house in Weston. My mother and a driver accordingly went there with him, where his wounds were dressed. He remained in Weston several weeks before he was able to stir about again, but he never fully recovered from the wounds, which eventually proved the cause of his death.[8]

Many times Isaac Cody was afraid to come home, as the Border Ruffians were looking for him, to finish what they had started, and he would hide out in the fields where his children took him food and medicine. His wife made a skirt, cape, and sunbonnet for him to wear so that he looked like a woman in case the Border Ruffians saw him.

William Cody would eventually become involved directly in the fight against the proslavery forces. In the winter of 1862, when Cody was 18 years old, he became a scout with the "Red Legs" and had many a "lively skirmish with the bushwhackers and Younger brothers. . . ."[9] Shortly after his mother died, he left home and joined the Kansas Seventh.

I soon left the home now rendered gloomy by the absence of her whom I had so tenderly loved and going to Leavenworth I entered upon a dissolute and reckless life — to my shame be it said — and associated with gamblers, drunkards, and bad characters generally. I continued my dissipation about two months, and was becoming a very "hard case." About this time the Seventh Kansas regiment, known as "Jennison's Jayhawkers," returned from the war, and re-enlisted and re-organized as veterans. Among them I met quite a number of my old comrades and neighbors, who tried to induce me to enlist and go South with them. I had no idea of doing anything of the kind; but one day, after having been under the influence of bad whisky, I awoke to find myself a soldier in the Seventh Kansas. I did not remember how or when I had enlisted, but I saw I was in for it, and that it would not do for me to endeavor to back out.[10]

William Cody traveled with the Seventh to fight in the South and then returned to fight General Sterling Price's army in Missouri, where he served as a scout. Cody related an interesting event that occurred.

I was still acting as a scout, when one day I rode ahead of the command, some considerable distance, to pick up all possible information concerning Price's movements. I was dressed in gray clothes, or Missouri jeans, and on riding up to a farm house and entering I saw a man, also dressed in gray costume, sitting at a table eating bread and milk. He looked up as I entered, and startled me by saying:

"You little rascal, what are you doing in those 'secesh' clothes?" Judge of my surprise when I recognized in the stranger my old friend and partner, Wild Bill, disguised as a Confederate officer.

"I ask you the same question, sir," said I, without the least hesitation.

"Hush! sit down and have some bread and milk, and we'll talk it all over afterwards," said he.

I accepted the invitation and partook of the refreshments. Wild Bill paid the woman of the house, and we went out to the gate where my horse was standing.

"Billy, my boy," said he "I am mighty glad to see you. I haven't seen or heard of you since we got busted on that St. Louis horse race."

"What are you doing here?" I asked.

"I am a scout under General McNeil. For the last few days I have been with General Marmaduke's division of Price's army, in disguise as a Southern officer from Texas, as you see me now," said he.

"That's exactly the kind of business that I am out on to-day," said I; "and I want to get some information concerning Price's movements."

"I'll give you all that I have;" and he then went on and told me all that he knew regarding Price's intentions, and the number and condition of his men. He then asked about my mother, and when he learned that she was dead he was greatly surprised and grieved; he thought a great deal of her, for she had treated him almost as one of her own children. He finally took out a package, which he had concealed about his person, and handing it to me he said:

"Here are some letters which I want you to give to General McNeil."

"All right," said I as I took them, "but where will I meet you again?"

"Never mind that," he replied; "I am getting so much valuable information that I propose to stay a little while longer in this disguise." Thereupon we shook hands and parted.[11]

Cody would see James "Wild Bill" Hickok again in another dramatic happening.

While both armies were drawn up in skirmish line near Fort Scott, Kansas, two men on horseback were seen rapidly leaving the Confederate lines, and suddenly they made a dash towards us. Instantly quick volleys were discharged from the Confederates, who also began a pursuit, and some five hundred shots were fired at the flying men. It was evident that they were trying to reach our lines, but when within about a quarter of a mile of us, one of them fell from his horse to rise no more. He had been fatally shot. His companion galloped on unhurt, and seven companies of our regiment charged out and met him, and checked his pursuers. The fugitive was dressed in Confederate uniform, and as he rode into our lines I recognized him as Wild Bill, the Union scout. He immediately sought Generals Pleasanton and McNeil, with whom he held a consultation. He told them that although Price made a bold showing on the front, by bringing all his men into view, yet he was really a great deal weaker than the appearance of his lines would indicate; and that he was then trying to cross a difficult stream four miles from Fort Scott.

It was late in the afternoon, but General Pleasanton immediately ordered an advance, and we charged in full force upon the rear of Price's army, and drove it before us for two hours.

If Wild Bill could have made his successful dash into our

James Butler "Wild Bill"
Hickok, *circa* 1858.
*Kansas State Historical
Society, Topeka*

lines earlier in the day, the attack would have been made sooner, and greater results might have been expected. The Confederates had suspected him of being a spy for two or three days, and had watched him too closely to allow an opportunity to get away from them sooner. His unfortunate companion who had been shot, was a scout from Springfield, Missouri, whose name I cannot now remember.

From this time on, Wild Bill and myself continued to scout together until Price's army was driven south of the Arkansas river and the pursuit abandoned.[12]

After the war, Cody continued to scout for the military in its Indian campaigns. He gained the nickname "Buffalo Bill" when he was hired to kill buffalo to feed the workers for the Kansas Pacific Railroad. By the late

1800s, the West, as Cody knew it, was changing, but he continued the myths of the West through his Wild West Show, which included

> . . . Indians, cow-boys, Mexican vaqueros, famous riders and expert lasso throwers, with accessories of stage coach, emigrant wagons, bucking horses and a herd of buffaloes, with which to give a realistic entertainment of wild life on the plains.[13]

Cody's show was very successful, not only in the United States but also in Europe, where he entertained royalty. Colonel W. F. Cody, the white-haired, regal leader of the Wild West Show had come a long way from little Billy Cody who was just starting to ride the Pony Express in 1859 when Abraham Lincoln came to Leavenworth.

Mary Delahay's stories of Lincoln begin before his visit to Leavenworth. She tells of being on the platform with the speakers during the last of the Lincoln-Douglas debates, on October 15, 1858, in Alton, Illinois, where the Delahay family was staying. Mark Delahay was in Kansas. Mary described it thus:

> Mr. George T. Brown, editor of the Alton Courier (later sergeant-at-arms of the United States senate during Mr. Lincoln's administration), was master of ceremonies on that occasion. He was a warm personal friend of the family, and knowing that the speakers also were our friends, he invited me to accompany him to the speaking, which I did, being the only little girl in the balcony. While Mr. Douglas spoke Mr. Lincoln held me in his arms, and while Mr. Lincoln spoke Mr. Douglas held me in his arms. I remember, also, that Mr. Lincoln received the largest number of bouquets.[14]

Later, when Mary was 16 and the Lincolns were in Washington, D.C., she attended a New Year's reception at the White House with her father and was awed at the formality and the brilliance of the occasion. She greatly admired Mrs. Lincoln and insisted that her father buy her a sun-shade like the First Lady's. She made many visits to Washington to see the

Lincolns and was invited to be their guest for six weeks and to make her debut into Washington Society from the White House. However, Mary's excitement over this opportunity was short-lived, as she was stricken by a sudden illness with a high fever, causing her long, luxurious hair to come out by the handful. She was unable to be seen in public, let alone presented in a debut. Before she could regain her previous beauty and accept the Lincolns' kind offer, the President was assassinated. With bitter disappointment, Mary knew her dream would never be fulfilled.[15]

Many people in Tonganoxie, Kansas, and the surrounding area believe that Abraham Lincoln also visited and stayed overnight in a nearby country home owned by Delahay. The two-story, ten-room house, known as "Lincoln's Rest," is approximately five miles northeast of Tonganoxie and about ten miles northwest of Leavenworth. According to local lore, Lincoln spent Saturday night and Sunday of his week's visit at the country home. Mrs. Cora Wellhouse Bullard told the story of her father, Judge Wellhouse, who had an apple orchard in the area and met Lincoln and Delahay in a buggy on the road near the Delahay farm in 1859. Delahay stopped his team and started to introduce Wellhouse to Lincoln when his guest said, "Hello, Wellhouse, what are you doing here?" Mr. Wellhouse and Lincoln had known each other in Illinois.[16]

If this story is true, the Delahay country home would be the only structure still standing in Kansas in which Lincoln stayed or spoke during his 1859 visit; all of the rest have since been destroyed by fire or torn down. An investigation shows the property was originally deeded to Mark Delahay in 1861 from the Leavenworth Pawnee and Western Railroad Company. If the property had been homesteaded, it would have been exempt from the land grant to the railroad and, in turn, could not have been deeded to Delahay. This would seem to preclude any possibility that the house could have been available when Lincoln visited in 1859. There might be the possibility that the deed was not officially registered until Kansas became a state in 1861.

According to Billy and Jean McGraw, one-time owners, the Delahay house was built in 1854. If this is true, the house then was not built by Delahay, as he did not come to Kansas until the spring of 1855. According to memoirs written by D. P. Hougland, he "rented Judge Delahay's farm, on the Big Stranger, and was living there at the time of the Lawrence massacre . . . ,"[17] which was August 1863. We do not know that Hougland was living in this same house, but if the property was purchased in 1861, a house could have been ready for occupancy by 1863.

Mary Delahay never mentioned Lincoln visiting another home in the area. She said in her memoirs, "Years have passed since Abraham Lincoln spent a week with us in our home in Leavenworth, Kansas." She described their home in town as being "in Kioway Street, third door from Third Street." The house is no longer standing. Mark Delahay purchased a home at 231 Third Avenue in Leavenworth, in 1863, which still stands. No other report corroborates or even mentions this story.

Mary's father, Mark Delahay, had moved his family to Leavenworth in March 1855. He brought with him from Illinois a printing press and other requisites for a printing office, and he became the editor of the *Kansas Territorial Register*. Delahay, at this time, seemed somewhat ambiguous about his politics. In 1855, when he was elected under the Topeka Constitution as a representative to Congress, the Lawrence *Herald of Freedom* called him a Douglas Democrat. Indeed, his early editorials were not as radically antislavery as they were by the winter of 1855, when his paper was sabotaged by the proslavery forces. Delahay was early on committed to Abraham Lincoln, the man, and, as the Republican Party formed and Lincoln moved from the Whig Party to the new Party, Delahay, always politically influenced by Lincoln, followed him.

On December 22, 1855, Delahay traveled to Lawrence for the nomination of officers under the Topeka Constitution. While he was absent, the office of the *Register* was broken into, and the press was demolished, carried to the river, and slid in through a hole cut in the ice. The type was strewed in the street, and the office would have been burned if not for the friendly intervention of Colonel William Russell of the overland freighter firm of Majors, Russell, and Waddell, who claimed the building as his own. Delahay and the other delegates were warned to leave the country, and a price of $500 was offered for Delahay's head. Being particularly vulnerable to the Western Ruffians while there was ice on the river, the men concluded "that prudence was the better part of valor," and departed New Year's Eve in a wagon, all armed to the teeth, driving overland through the nights, and spending the days in Indian huts. They reached Jefferson City, Missouri, where they took the railroad to St. Louis, thence east. The Delahay family could not follow until navigation was open on the Missouri River. They subsequently returned to Kansas, in 1857, and Mark established another paper in Wyandotte, the *Wyandotte Reporter*. He practiced law and ran a hotel for a year or two, while the boom lasted there, and then he returned to Leavenworth.[18]

Lincoln referred to this event in a speech he gave at Bloomington, Illinois, on May 28, 1856, reported by the *Illinois State Register*.

> In the evening a meeting was held in front of Pike House, and several speeches were made. The speakers were Lincoln, Washburne, Palmer, Swett, Lovejoy and Wentworth.
>
> Lincoln led off; said he didn't expect to make a speech then; that he had prepared himself for one, but 'twas not suitable at that time; but that after awhile he would make them a most excellent one. Notwithstanding, he kept on speaking, told his old story about the fence (meaning Missouri restriction) being torn down and the cattle eating up the crops, then talked about the outrages in Kansas; said a man couldn't think, dream or breathe of a free state there, but what he was kicked, cuffed, shot down and hung; he then got very pathetic over poor Delahay and Tom Shoemaker. By the way, Mr. Register, I wonder if any one in this community knows Delahay and Shoemaker; if so we pass them and also Lincoln's speech, and come next to that of Washburne, which was celebrated only for the vehement and uproarious manner with which it was delivered.[19]

Lincoln was referring to Delahay's paper being destroyed, and to Thomas Shoemaker, a free-stater, who had been appointed receiver of the Land Office for Kansas in 1855. Shoemaker was removed in October 1856, then in April 1857, he was killed at Leavenworth in a barroom brawl growing out of a political argument.[20]

According to Mary Delahay, one evening during Lincoln's stay at their home, a half-dozen gentlemen were invited to dinner to meet Lincoln; among them were Judge Pettit, Marcus J. Parrott, S. N. Latta, and General James H. Lane. Mary assisted her mother in the dining room and overheard the men's conversation concerning politics.

> My father rose to carve, as was his habit, and pausing, knife in hand, remarked, "Gentlemen, I tell you Mr. Lincoln will be our next President." Mr. Lincoln replied, "Oh Delahay, hush." My father retorted, "I feel it, and I mean it." After this prediction was verified, in Kansas it was spoken of as Delahay's prophecy.[21]

Even though Mary said that James Lane met Lincoln at her house, Lane says in a note included in a Delahay letter to Lincoln dated February 17, 1860, ". . . I have never met you and yet I feel that you are an old acquaintance and I may add friend. . . ."[22] One would not be surprised that Lane would have been in attendance when Lincoln came, since he was such a key player in the Party, but evidently he was not. Clearly Lane and Delahay were friends and had shared the free-stater fight politically. John Speer, Lane's biographer, reported an incident that involved Lane and Delahay in the raising of funds to benefit Lane's campaign to be elected as the first Senator from Kansas. Speer had purchased a newspaper in Lawrence to promote Lane and needed $500 to keep the employees working until after the election. Lane went to Leavenworth (according to William Connelley's biography he walked the 35 miles in knee-deep snow[23]) and to his friend Delahay to raise the funds. Delahay later told the story to Speer:

> Christmas night, at 12 o'clock, a rap was at my door. I put out my head, and the wind blew so hard and the snow flew so thick I could see nothing. "Who's there?" said I, "and what do you want such a night as this?" "Lane; come down." I came. "Are you crazy, Lane?" said I. "No. Speer has bought the Lawrence Republican." "That is good. But what of it?" "He wants $500, to keep the hands from striking till the paper can earn something." "Now I know you are crazy. Neither of us can raise a dollar." "I have a plan, Mark. You know these Fort

Leavenworth officers never bought a bushel of corn from a Free-State man. You go to the Fort, and tell them that your cousin, Abraham Lincoln, wants you to go to Springfield, and you may have to go to Washington, and you want to sell them $500 worth of corn. Ham. Johnson had the corn. Tell them that, Mark, and you will think that every mule around the Fort is braying for corn." I told the story, and I had a check for $500 before I told them where to find the corn.[24]

Delahay evidently traveled with Lane, at least part of the time, on his trip to the North to raise funds for Kansas. Delahay related to Speer this incident that occurred in New York.

Hon. Mark W. Delahay, United States District Judge for the State of Kansas, told me an amusing story of their appearance together in New York, hungry, in a restaurant, Lane penniless, and Delahay with only seventy-five cents, begging his co-partner to moderate his appetite for another meal; but they left that table without the means for a plate of soup. "How on earth," said I, "did you get out of that great city?" "Oh," said Delahay, laughing, "Lane hunted up a committee, replenished our treasury, and the committee got out bills, and rented a hall with such good results that they sent us on our way rejoicing, for an assault on Democratic Connecticut!" [25]

Delahay's prophecy would come true and Lincoln, as President, would appoint Mark Delahay as Surveyor General of Kansas and Nebraska, and later as Federal District Court Judge of Kansas. Lincoln selected Delahay over the protests of the Kansas Bar and press. As one opponent protested, "There is not a respectable lawyer in the State that is not absolutely shocked at the appointment."[26] People from out of state were also opposed, as noted by the collector of Internal Revenue Jackson Grimshaw, of Quincy, Illinois, in an appeal to Senator Lyman Trumbull:

Will the Senate confirm that miserable man Delahay for Judge in Kansas. The appointment is disgraceful to the

President who knew Delahay and all his faults, but the disgrace will be greater if the Senate confirms him. He is no lawyer, could not try a case properly even in a Justice's Court, and has no character. Mr. Buchanan in his worst days never made so disgraceful an appointment to the bench.[27]

Another critical newspaper editor reflecting on Delahay's limited legal learning made the salty comment that ". . . the only bench Delahay was qualified to sit on was one with a hole in it."[28]

Delahay's opponents were vindicated when on March 3, 1873, due to "flagrant conduct," that included being drunk on the bench, articles of impeachment were brought against Judge Delahay and he resigned.[29]

In spite of the criticism of Delahay, Lincoln continued the long relationship that he had established with Delahay many years earlier. Lincoln much earlier had made his friendship for Delahay known in this letter, written after his very successful visit to the East where he made the famous Cooper Institute speech.

*Springfield, Ills —*
*mar. 16th, 1860.*

*Dear Delahay —*

*I've just returned from the East — Before leaving, I received your letter of Feb. 6th; and on my return I find those of the 17th and 19th with Genl. Lane's note inclosed in one of them.*

*I sincerely wish you could be elected one of the first Senators for Kansas; but how to help you I do not know. (Even) If it were permissable for me to interfere, I am not personally acquainted with a single Member of your Legislature. If my known friendship for you could be of any advantage, that friendship was abundantly manifested by me last December while in Kansas. If any member had written me, as you say some have Trumbull, I would very readily answer him. I shall write Trumbull on this subject at this sitting.*

*I understood, while in Kansas, that the State Legislature will not meet until the State is admitted — was that the right understanding?*

*As to your kind wishes for myself, allow me to say I cannot enter the ring on the money basis — first, because, in the main, it is wrong; and secondly, I have not and cannot get, the money. I say, in the main, the use of money is wrong: but for certain objects, in a political contest, the use of some is both right and indispensable. With me, as with yourself, this long struggle has been one of great pecuniary loss. I now distinctly say this — if you shall be appointed a delegate to Chicago, I will furnish one hundred dollars to bear the expenses of the trip.*

*Present my respects to Genl. Lane; and say to him, I shall be pleased to hear from him at any time. Your friend as ever, A. Lincoln.*

*P.S. I have not yet taken the newspaper slip to the Journal. I shall do that tomorrow; and then send you the paper as requested.*

*A. L*[30]

Delahay was not appointed as a delegate to Chicago, but in a letter dated April 14, 1860, Lincoln says:

*... I see by the despaches that since you wrote, Kansas has appointed Delegates and instructed them for Seward. Don't stir them up to anger, but come along to the convention, & I will do as I said about expenses. Yours as ever*

*A Lincoln*[31]

Delahay had worked with and for Lincoln politically in Illinois. He was editor of a Whig paper and, through his articles, was able to assist Lincoln in defeating another politician who attempted to supplant Lincoln as Congressman. According to Delahay, ". . . in a letter Lincoln did me the high honor of ascribing his success to my efforts."[32]

This political partnership continued when Delahay came to Kansas, where he was Lincoln's voice. Lincoln's letters show that they stayed in touch about the political events in the state from the time Delahay had arrived.

Lincoln evidently valued Delahay's opinion, as he sought it on numerous occasions. He also enlisted Delahay's help in campaigning for him. Even though he was not a delegate, Delahay was very involved, behind the scenes, in swaying people to Lincoln in the Presidential Convention of 1860. And after Lincoln's nomination, Delahay and Lane went to Indiana and Illinois to work in the doubtful districts that Lincoln carried in the November election. In appreciation, Lincoln gave Delahay a large banner he had received during the Lincoln-Douglas debates.[33] After Lincoln was elected, he asked for Delahay's opinion on appointments that he made in Kansas.

> M. W. Delahay, Esq.                                 Executive Mansion
>
> My dear Sir                                            March 13, 1861
>
> You will start for Kansas before I see you again; and when I saw you a moment this morning, I forgot to ask you about some of the Kansas appointments, which I intended to do. If you care much about them, you can write, as I think I shall not make the appointments just yet. Yours in haste.
>
>                                                     A. Lincoln[34]

In Delahay's response, he asked for and received the appointment of Surveyor General of Kansas. According to Mary Delahay, Lincoln offered her father the Chilean mission, which he declined, before Lincoln appointed him to the Surveyor General position.

Delahay's connection to Lincoln was known, especially in Kansas, and people asked him to intercede for them with the President. Delahay relates the story of the discharge of a young man from the draft, the son of Colonel Andrew Ege, a slaveholder who had earlier responded with disfavor to Lincoln's speech at Troy, Kansas:

He had been a resident of Arkansas when the war broke

out, and, like many others similarly situated, had joined the rebel army. His father at much trouble and expense had gotten him out of the service, and inside of our lines, the son giving his parole not again to join the army, or aid the rebellion. This parole was given upon the promise of the father, that he should not be compelled to take up arms on the side of the Union. The son returned to his old home in Maryland and was there drafted. The father felt in honor bound to make good his promise, as his son held him responsible for it, and went to Washington to secure his release. Upon his behalf I went to the President, stated the facts, and added that the young man was the son of a gentleman who replied to a speech made by Mr. Lincoln at Troy, in Doniphan county, Kansas, 1859. The father had not wished the President to know this, fearing that it would operate against the accomplishment of his mission; but I knew the generosity of Mr. Lincoln's character well enough to be certain that the fact of the applicant having been an old opponent, would tell in his favor with him, and that no personal reasons would be permitted for a moment to interfere with his natural bearing or leaning to justice and clemency. As I anticipated, Mr. Lincoln told me at once to prepare the papers in the form of affidavits, and the young man was immediately discharged. I mention this circumstance to show that he never treasured up anything personal against a political opponent, and was not the man to retaliate upon such, but on the contrary was so utterly above any vindictive feelings, that he was perhaps more easily reached for favors by his political enemies, than by his life-long friends.[35]

Delahay was accurate in that Lincoln never hesitated to appoint an opponent to a position if he was qualified. He appointed William H. Seward and Salmon P. Chase to his cabinet, both of whom had been political opponents. In the same vein, he seemed to be able to continue a relationship with a friend in spite of errors in judgment or behavior. Delahay certainly benefited from Lincoln's charitable nature. Delahay had believed in Lincoln's ability to be elected and had committed to it early on. Certainly Lincoln appreciated and rewarded Delahay's political shrewdness and his confidence in Lincoln's political abilities.

Mark Delahay died at age 61 on May 8, 1879, and is buried with his family in the Mt. Muncie Cemetery in Leavenworth. Even though Delahay was unable to maintain his rise to the top, in a sense, his oldest daughter Julia accomplished it in his stead when she married Thomas Osborn, who became the sixth Governor of the state of Kansas.

Julia Delahay Osborn.  *Kansas State Historical Society, Topeka*

Another young girl who was only a few years older than Mary Delahay when she met Abraham Lincoln was Vinnie Ream. In 1863, Vinnie's abilities as a sculptress were recognized by Clark Mills, a leading artist in Washington, D.C. He was so impressed with her talent that he took her as a pupil. By 1864, some of Vinnie's friends had convinced President Lincoln to sit for her, so that she might model a bust of him. At first reluctant, he was convinced when he learned she was a poor, struggling girl with much talent. He sat for her daily for a half hour, for five months. Vinnie's last sitting with Lincoln was on April 14, 1865. The President left the session early to take Mrs. Lincoln to the theater. It was the last sitting for any artist before his death. Vinnie, who was only 16 years old at the time, described herself and Mr. Lincoln.

I was the merest slip of a child, weighing less than 90 pounds, and the contrast between the rawboned man and me was indeed great. I sat demurely in my corner and begged Mr. Lincoln not to allow me to disturb him. It seemed that he used this half hour as time of relaxation, for he always left instructions that no one was to be admitted during that time. He seemed to find a strange sort of companionship in being with me, although we talked but little. His favorite son Willie, had but just died, and this had been the greatest personal sorrow in a life that was mostly sorrowful. I made him think of Willie. He often said so and as often wept.

I remember him especially in two attitudes. The first was with his great form slouched down into a chair at his desk, his head bowed upon his chest, deeply thoughtful. I think he was with his generals on the battlefields, appraising the horrible sacrifices brought upon his people and the nation.

The second was at the window watching for Willie, for he had always watched the boy playing every afternoon at that window. Sometimes great tears rolled down his cheeks. . . .

I think that history is particularly correct in writing about Abraham Lincoln to describe him as a man of unfathomable sorrow. That was the lasting impression I always had of him. . . . He never told a funny story and he rarely smiled.

He had been painted and modeled before, but when he learned that I was poor, he granted me the sittings for no other purpose than that I was a poor girl. Had I been the greatest sculptor in the world, I am sure that he would have refused at that time.[36]

After President Lincoln died, Congress offered a commission of $10,000 for a statue of the assassinated President. Vinnie Ream's bust of Lincoln had received enough attention that she was encouraged to apply for the commission. Her application, however, received much criticism; many thought she was too young to produce a quality work and questioned her close relations with gentlemen of Washington. Women were the most critical of Vinnie — especially Mrs. Jane Grey Swisshelm, editor of the *Pittsburgh Saturday Visitor*. Swisshelm, backing the application of a Harriet Hosmer of Massachusetts, was particularly vicious.

> . . . [*Vinnie sees*] members at their lodgings or in the recep-
> tion room at the Capitol, urges her claims fluently and confi-
> dently, sits in the galleries in a conspicuous position and in her
> most bewitching dress . . . and so carries the day over Powers,
> Crawford and Hosmer, and who not?[37]

Vinnie was not intimidated by the Washington society that criticized
her, and she appealed to men of influence for help. She was small, pretty,
and persuasive; her charming personality and her long dark, curling hair
were not impediments to her cause. She was able to enlist the aid of President Andrew Johnson, members of his cabinet, members of the Legislature, General George Armstrong Custer, and General William Tecumseh
Sherman. Her lobbying efforts were successful and, in 1866, she was
awarded the $10,000
contract to do a full-
size marble statue of
Lincoln for the Capitol
rotunda. Vinnie was
only 18 years old at the
time, and was the first
woman to ever be
awarded such a federal
commission.

Vinnie Ream was
born in 1847 in Mad-
ison, Wisconsin, to
Robert and Lavinia
Ream. By 1854, Robert
Ream had accepted an
assignment in Kansas
as a Clerk to Surveyor
General John Calhoun.
The family settled first
in Wyandotte, where
they managed the

Vinnie Ream.                        *Kansas State Historical Society, Topeka*

The marble statue of Abraham Lincoln, by Vinnie Ream, in the Capitol rotunda.
*Kansas State Historical Society, Topeka*

Eldridge House Hotel. The Reams sent Vinnie and her sister Mary away
to school in St. Joseph, Missouri, supposedly because of fear of Indian
attack. Curiously enough, Vinnie may have first seen Abraham Lincoln in
Leavenworth, during his visit there. In 1857, when Vinnie was ten years
old, Robert Ream had moved his family to Leavenworth where they lived
until late in 1859, when they moved to Arkansas.

After the death of Surveyor General Calhoun, the Reams had managed
a hotel in Leavenworth — the Shawnee House, located between Main
and 2nd Streets on Shawnee — where Robert Ream was said to have
". . . slung hash for patrons and chased bedbugs."[38] The girls were again
sent away to school, this time to Christian College at Columbia, Missouri,
where Vinnie excelled in music, art, and writing. At Christian College she
wrote a poem entitled *My Kansas Home.*

> My Kansas Home, I long for thee,
> Thy woodland dells and murmuring rills
> Thy songs of melody and love,
> Thy rivers broad and grand old hills,
> I long for hours of joy that passed
> Beneath thy smiling skies of blue,
> To be again with those I love
> Whose hearts for me beat kind and true.
>
> I long to clamber o'er thy steeps,
> To cull thy fragrant wild-wood flowers,
> To wreath them into garlands fair,
> And twine them 'mong my leafy bowers;
> I long to view thy prairies wild,
> And bound o'er them with footstep free;
> To watch the grassy billows heave,
> As the winds play o'er the emerald sea.
>
> Though varied are the scenes of life,
> Where'er my footsteps chance to roam,
> My thoughts will fondly turn to thee —
> My wild, yet lovely Kansas home.
> When through the misty sky of morn
> The golden sunlight streams around,
> With brightest colors painting o'er
> Fair nature from the sky to ground,

I think of thee, My Kansas Home,
And how among the woodland bowers
I oft have watched the morning dawn
And sunlight gild the dewy flowers;
I think of thee, when o'er the earth
The sun's last lingering rays are thrown,
And warblers hush their melodies,
And I am left to muse alone.

When twilight shades come stealing on,
And flowers bathe their heads in dew,
When fire-flies dance upon the lawn,
And stars smile from the Heaven's deep blue,
When fairy moonlight's silver rays
Are streaming o'er the earth below,
As if they'd lighten all our cares,
And banish all our thoughts of woe,

I think of thee, my Kansas Home,
And of the hours of joy and love
That fleeted by among the bowers,
When stars seemed laughing from above;
And of my pleasant wanderings,
When moonlight shadows fell around,
All checkering o'er with silver lines
The tree-tops and the grassy ground.

I dream of thee when silently
The stars their nightly vigils keep,
When earth is shrouded in deep gloom.
And every form is wrapped in sleep;
I dream that I am with my friends,
A wanderer no longer roam,
That I am sharing of the joys,
That cluster 'round my Kansas Home.[39]

While in Leavenworth, the Reams became acquainted with a young newspaperman, Edmund Ross. Their acquaintance with him would continue after they moved to Washington, D.C. In 1861, Ross was

Major Edmund G. Ross.
*Kansas State Historical Society, Topeka*

appointed to serve the remainder of Senator James Lane's term, after the Senator's suicide. Ross boarded with the Reams in Washington and became fast friends with Vinnie, who had been given a studio in the basement of the Capitol to work on the contracted statue.

In 1858, Edmund Ross, an ardent abolitionist and true pioneer, had driven an ox team to Kansas as the head of an abolitionist party of 300. A man of strong opinions, who had fought honorably in the Civil War, he was well respected in the U.S. Senate. His future was promising, until the attempted impeachment of President Andrew Johnson. The Congressional leaders who were determined to impeach Johnson counted on the vote of the Kansas Senator, but Ross refused to commit. In an attempt to secure enough votes, politicians harassed not only Ross for a positive vote, but pressured Vinnie in her studio to influence him to vote for impeachment. But Ross refused to discuss the case and silently listened to the proceedings of the trial. The day before the vote, Kansas Senators Ross and Pomeroy received a joint telegram from Daniel R. Anthony of Leavenworth, and "1,000 others of our truest and best men," who wrote, "Kansas has heard the evidence and demands the conviction of the President."[40]

Pomeroy pressured Ross to vote for impeachment. The impeachment politicians had believed to the end that they had Ross' vote. But when the vote was cast, Ross voted against impeachment, and it failed by one vote. Ross received another telegram from Kansas calling him a skunk.[41] He became the object of ridicule and abuse by his fellow party leaders, who blamed him for the lost vote. A telegram from Daniel Anthony in Leavenworth said, "Kansas repudiates you as she does all perjurers and snakes."[42] A Kansas Supreme Court Justice offered, "The rope with which Judas Iscariot hanged himself is lost, but Jim Lane's pistol is at your service."[43] Kansans, who accused Ross of bribery, were joined by Senator Benjamin Butler who snarled, "Tell the damned scoundrel that if he wants money, there is a bushel of it here to be had!"[44] When Ross was refused another term by an angry Kansas Legislature and returned to his adopted home state, he was met with the same kind of hatred and abuse he had endured in Washington, D.C. Ross later spoke of his experience.

> I don't believe there was a bypath or a country road in all the North so obscure but that it was lighted by burning effigies of me after that vote was cast. No man can ever know the struggle that vote cost me. I went into the trail a very radical Republican. I had been through all the bitterness of the slavery fight in Kansas. Rebellion was hateful to me in all its forms. The tentative governments established by President Johnson only added to the intensity of my feelings. I had strenuously opposed the President's policy throughout. But when I took the oath, not as a senator, but as a judge and juror, to give Andrew Johnson a fair and impartial trial, that oath meant to me what it said. I determined to throw off every prejudice and predilection and observe that oath notwithstanding I was opposed to the President's policy and earnestly desired the office rid of him. The conviction was slowly borne in upon me during the long trial that there was too much politics in the prosecution. As the end was reached, I was forced to the conclusion that while Mr. Johnson had been very arbitrary and utterly tactless, stubborn and hard-headed, yet he was in no wise criminal, and had nowhere crossed the line marking the limits of his constitutional rights, but had sought only to obtain a judicial determination of all disputed questions in the supreme court.
>
> The personality of Mr. Johnson had little to do with my

action. I did what I thought was right — what I thought under the circumstances. I thought I saw the beginning of insidious and disintegrating revolutionary forces in the movement for his impeachment.

Had I voted for impeachment, the indications were that I might have remained in the Senate as long as I wished. I seemed to have the ruling element of the state behind me. . . . Then they left me, with every other thing I possessed. From that time on the dogs wouldn't bark at me. I have suffered the effects of that act, done in the highest sense of public duty, every since, financially as well as every other way. I have been a wandering . . . printer pretty much ever since.[45]

Harassed and disillusioned, Ross left Kansas in 1882 and moved to New Mexico, living his last days in poverty on a small fruit farm on the edge of Albuquerque.

William Tecumseh Sherman.
*Kansas State Historical Society, Topeka*

Another actor in the drama of Abraham Lincoln's life was also in Leavenworth in 1859. William Tecumseh Sherman came to Leavenworth in September 1858 at the urging of his brother-in-law, Thomas Ewing, Jr., who, in partnership with his father and brother, Hugh, had purchased land in town and in the country. Thomas and Hugh also owned a law firm. Sherman's father-in-law offered him the general management of his property, and the brothers offered to make him a co-partner in their legal endeavors. Sherman picks up the story:

> Accordingly, about the 1st of September, I started for Kansas, stopping a couple of weeks in St. Louis, and reached Leavenworth. I found about two miles below the fort, on the river-bank, where in 1851 was a tangled thicket, quite a handsome and thriving city, growing rapidly in rivalry with Kansas City, and St. Joseph, Missouri. After looking about and consulting with friends, among them my classmate Major Stewart Van Vliet, quartermaster at the fort, I concluded to accept the proposition of Mr. Ewing, and accordingly the firm of Sherman & Ewing was duly announced, and our services to the public offered as attorneys-at-law.
>
> We had an office on Main Street, between Shawnee and Delaware, on the second floor, over the office of Hampton Denman, Esq., mayor of the city. This building was a mere shell, and our office was reached by a stairway on the outside. Although in the course of my military reading I had studied a few of the ordinary law-books, such as Blackstone, Kent, Starkie, etc., I did not presume to be a lawyer; but our agreement was that Thomas Ewing, Jr., a good and thorough lawyer, should manage all business in the courts, while I gave attention to collections, agencies for houses and lands, and such business as my experience in banking had qualified me for. Yet, as my name was embraced in a law-firm, it seemed to me proper to take out a license. Accordingly, one day when United States Judge Lecompte was in our office, I mentioned the matter to him; he told me to go down to the clerk of his court, and he would give me the license. I inquired what examination I would have to submit to, and he replied, "None at all;" he would admit me on the ground of general intelligence.
>
> During that summer we got our share of the business of the profession, then represented by several eminent law-firms, embracing names that have since flourished in the Senate, and in the higher courts of the country. But the most lucrative single case was given me by my friend Major Van Vliet, who employed me to go to Fort Riley, one hundred and thirty-six

miles west of Fort Leavenworth, to superintend the repairs to
the military road. For this purpose he supplied me with a
four-mule ambulance and driver. The country was then sparse-
ly settled, and quite as many Indians were along the road as
white people; still there were embryo towns all along the route,
and a few farms sprinkled over the beautiful prairies. On reaching Indianola, near Topeka, I found everybody down with the
chills and fever. My own driver became so shaky that I had to
act as driver and cook. But in due season I reconnoitred the
road, and made contracts for repairing some bridges, and for
cutting such parts of the road as needed it. I then returned to
Fort Leavenworth, and reported, receiving a fair compensation.

Mrs. Sherman and children arrived out in November, and we
spent the winter very comfortably in the house of Thomas
Ewing, Jr., on the corner of Third and Pottawottamie Streets.
On the 1st of January, 1859, Daniel McCook, Esq., was admitted to membership in our firm, which became Sherman,
Ewing & McCook. Our business continued to grow, but, as the
income hardly sufficed for three such expensive personages, I
continued to look about for something more certain and prof-
itable, and during the spring undertook for the Hon. Thomas
Ewing, of Ohio, to open a farm on a large tract of land he
owned on Indian Creek, forty miles west of Leavenworth, for
the benefit of his grand-nephew, Henry Clark, and his grand-
niece, Mrs. Walker. These arrived out in the spring, by which
time I had caused to be erected a small frame dwelling-house,
a barn, and fencing for a hundred acres. This helped to pass
away time, but afforded little profit.

. . . I must explain a little matter of which I have seen an
account in print, complimentary or otherwise of the firm of
Sherman, Ewing & McCook, more especially of the senior partner.

One day, as I sat in our office, an Irish man came in and said
he had a case and wanted a lawyer. I asked him to sit down and
give me the points of his case, all the other members of the firm
being out. Our client stated that he had rented a lot of an Irish
landlord for five dollars a month; that he had erected thereon a
small frame shanty, which was occupied by his family; that he

had paid his rent regularly up to a recent period, but to his house he had appended a shed which extended over a part of an adjoining vacant lot belonging to the same landlord, for which he was charged two and a half dollars a month, which he refused to pay. The consequence was, that his landlord had for a few months declined even his five dollars monthly rent until the arrears amounted to about seventeen dollars, for which I took notes, and a fee of five dollars in advance, and in due order I placed the notes in the hands of McCook, and thought no more of it.

A month or so after, our client rushed into the office and said his case had been called at Judge Gardner's (I think), and he wanted his lawyer right away. I sent him up to the Circuit Court, Judge Pettit's, for McCook, but he soon returned, saying he could not find McCook, and accordingly I hurried with him up to Judge Gardner's office, intending to ask a continuance, but I found our antagonist there, with his lawyer and witnesses, and Judge Gardner would not grant a continuance, so of necessity I had to act, hoping that at every minute McCook would come. But the trial proceeded regularly to its end; we were beaten, and judgment was entered against our client for the amount claimed, and costs. As soon as the matter was explained to McCook, he said "execution" could not be taken for ten days, and, as our client was poor, and had nothing on which the landlord could levy but his house, McCook advised him to get his neighbors together, to pick up the house, and carry it on to another vacant lot, belonging to a non-resident, so that even the house could not be taken in execution. Thus the grasping landlord, though successful in his judgment, failed in the execution, and our client was abundantly satisfied.[46]

William T. Sherman left Leavenworth in July 1859, before Lincoln's visit in December of that year, but their paths would cross a few years later when Sherman would become one of the most important Union Generals of the Civil War and Abraham Lincoln would become his Commander-in-Chief.

Sherman met Lincoln for the first time shortly after Lincoln became President in 1861. Sherman was, at that time, serving as the Superintendent of the Louisiana Seminary of Learning and Military Academy at Alexandria. He was in Washington, D.C., to visit his brother, Senator John Sherman, who had come to Kansas on a Congressional committee to investigate the situation during the Lecompton Constitution debates in 1858. Sherman described their meeting:

> One day, John Sherman took me with him to see Mr. Lincoln. He walked into the room where the secretary to the President now sits, we found the room full of people, and Mr. Lincoln sat at the end of the table, talking with three or four gentlemen, who soon left. John walked up, and shook hands, and took a chair near him, holding in his hand some papers referring to minor appointments in the State of Ohio, which formed the subject of conversation. Mr. Lincoln took the papers, said he would refer them to the proper heads of departments, and would be glad to make the appointments asked for, if not already promised. John then turned to me, and said, "Mr. President, this is my brother, Colonel Sherman, who is just up from Louisiana, he may give you some information you want." "Ah!" said Mr. Lincoln, "how are they getting along down there?" I said, "They think they are getting along swimmingly — they are preparing for war." "Oh, well!" said he, "I guess we'll manage to keep house." I was silenced, said no more to him, and we soon left. I was sadly disappointed, and remember that I broke out on John, d—ning the politicians generally, saying, "You have got things in a hell of a fix, and you may get them out as you best can," adding that the country was sleeping on a volcano that might burst forth at any minute. . . .[47]

Sherman, at the beginning of the war, thought that it was an unnecessary conflict between the States and was disappointed in the politicians and President Lincoln for not solving the situation peaceably. After the war, his opinion of Lincoln, like so many others, had changed considerably. Sherman had finished his famous march through the South when he met with Lincoln for the last time. In his memoirs he described their meeting.

> After I had been with him (Gen. Grant) an hour or so, he

remarked that the President, Mr. Lincoln, was then on board the steamer River Queen, lying at the wharf, and he proposed that we should call and see him. We walked down to the wharf, went on board, and found Mr. Lincoln alone, in the after-cabin. He remembered me perfectly and at once engaged in a most interesting conversation. He was full of curiosity about the many incidents of our great march, which had reached him officially and through the newspapers, and seemed to enjoy very much the more ludicrous parts — about the "bummers," and their devices to collect food and forage when the outside world supposed us to be starving; but at the same time he expressed a good deal of anxiety lest some accident might happen to the army in North Carolina (Goldsboro') during my absence. . . . I assured him that General Schofield was fully competent to command in my absence; that I was going to start back that very day.

I know, when I left him, that I was more than ever impressed by his kindly nature, his deep and earnest sympathy with the afflictions of the whole people, resulting from the war, and by the march of hostile armies through the South; and that his earnest desire seemed to be to end the war speedily, without more bloodshed or devastation, and to restore all the men of both sections to their homes. In the language of his second inaugural address, he seemed to have "charity for all, malice toward none," and, above all, an absolute faith in the courage, manliness, and integrity of the armies in the field. When at rest or listening, his legs and arms seemed to hang almost lifeless, and his face was care-worn and haggard; but, the moment he began to talk, his face lightened up, his tall form, as it were, unfolded, and he was the very impersonation of good-humor and fellowship. The last words I recall as addressed to me were that he would feel better when I was back at Goldsboro'. We parted at the gangway of the River Queen, about noon of March 28th, and I never saw him again. Of all the men I ever met, he seemed to possess more of the elements of greatness, combined with goodness, than any other.[48]

The four men who had been members of the law firm in Leavenworth would become Generals in the Union Army during the Civil War. Thomas Ewing, Jr., would be an integral player in the Free-State Party, a member of the Frontier Guard that went to Washington to protect President Lincoln, and would become the first Chief Justice of Kansas in 1861. William Tecumsch Sherman is remembered in Leavenworth for establishing the School of Application for Cavalry and Infantry that would become the U.S. Army Command and General Staff College at Fort Leavenworth. Leavenworth also has the distinction of being the only place Sherman ever practiced law and where he lost what may have been the only case he ever tried.

When Mark Delahay wrote the letter of invitation to Lincoln that was signed by 52 Leavenworth merchants and businessmen, Jonas Wollman was one of the names on the letter. Jonas and Betty Wollman were friends of the Delahays and also firm abolitionists. Jonas had aroused the wrath of the proslavery forces when he rented the loft over his store to Mark Delahay's antislavery newspaper, the *Territorial Register*. When Delahay's press was dumped in the river, the U.S. Marshal took Jonas and Betty into protective custody while he made his investigation. The Wollmans, like the Codys and many other abolitionist families, paid the price for their viewpoints, according to author Joan Ferris Curran.

> Three times the Wollmans were detained by "border ruffians," and once Betty and her infant daughter Rosa were held by them for more than a day. On another occasion, when Betty sensed an imminent raid, she and Rosa escaped in a rowboat to the town of Weston, Missouri. Still later, she saw her neighbor shot to death as he stood next to his wife in their front doorway.[49]

William Connelley, in his *History of Kansas*, reports what appears to be the same incident. According to Connelley, William Phillips, a lawyer and a Free-Stater, protested against the illegal voting of the Missourians in the Territorial election. As punishment for his offensive, he was kidnaped and taken to Weston where he was tarred and feathered. Mounted on a rail, he was carried through the streets to the accompaniment of the rabble,

Betty Wollman (1836-1927), wife of Jonas Wollman — Kansas' early settlers and abolitionists.
*Kansas State Historical Society, Topeka*

ringing bells, and beating on old pans. At the St. George Hotel, Dr. Parsons' old slave, Joe, was forced to auction off Phillips to the highest bidder. There were no bidders, and Joe "bid in" the lawyer for one cent. Phillips was told to leave town, but refused. During the purge of Free-State men from Leavenworth on September 1, 1856, his house was attacked. Phillips defended himself and killed two of the Ruffians. He, in turn, was shot many times by the Border Ruffians and fell dead in his doorway in front of his wife.[50]

According to family history, Abraham Lincoln visited Jonas and Betty Wollman's home when he came to Leavenworth.

While there, he cradled young Henry Wollman in his arms. Betty was impressed by Mr. Lincoln's quiet and positive manner, and when he left she commented to her husband, "There is a great man, and I tell you that someday he will be President of the United States." She repeated this prediction to others, but no one took her seriously.[51]

Robert Bloch, a descendant of the Wollman family, shares his ancestor's interest in Abraham Lincoln. In the summer of 1999, Robert provided a new marker for the grave of Mary Owens Vineyard, buried in Pleasant Ridge Cemetery near Weston, Missouri, across the river from Leavenworth, Kansas. The marker reads:

ABRAHAM LINCOLN'S OTHER MARY

MARY OWENS VINEYARD

1808 —— 1877

HERE LIES MARY OWENS VINEYARD

WHO REJECTED ABRAHAM LINCOLN'S

PROPOSAL OF MARRIAGE IN 1837.

Mary Owens, sometimes known as Lincoln's "other Mary," was originally from Kentucky but met Lincoln in Illinois through her sister. She was a tall, handsome woman, well educated and intellectual. Lincoln's interest in Mary is evident in the letters he wrote to her, the first written when Lincoln attended the Illinois Legislature in December 1836. (The letter is part of a manuscript owned by James G. Vineyard, Kansas City, Missouri, grandson of Mary Owens. The manuscript is damaged in spots; portions of the text now illegible are bracketed.)

*Vandalia, Decer. 13, 1836*

*Mary*

*I have been sick ever since my arrival here, or I should have written sooner. It is but little difference, however, as I have* very little even yet to write. And more, the longer I can avoid the mortification of looking in the Post Office for your letter and not finding it, the better. You see I am mad about that old letter yet. I don't like verry well to risk you again. I'll try you once more any how.

The new State House is not yet finished, and consequently the legislature is doing little or nothing. The Governor delivered an inflamitory political Message, and it is expected there will be some sparring between the parties about [it as] soon as the two Houses get to business. Taylor [deliv]ered up his petitions for the New County to one of [our me]mbers this morning. I am told that he dispairs [of its] success on account of all the members from Morg[an C]ounty opposing it. There are names enough on the petition[,] I think, to justify the members from our county in going for it; but if the members from Morgan oppose it, which they [say] they will, the chance will be bad.

Our chance to [take th]e seat of Government to Springfield is better than I ex[pected]. An Internal Improvement Convention was held here since we met, which recommended a loan of several milli[ons] of dollars on the faith of the State to construct Rail Roads. Some of the legislature are for it[,] and some against it; which has the majority I can not tell. There is great strife and struggling for the office of U.S. Senator here at this time. It is probable we shall ease their pains in a few days. The opposition men have no candidate of their own, and consequently they smile as complacently at the angry snarls of the contending Van Buren candidates and their respective friends, as the christain does at Satan's rage. you recollect I mentioned in the outset of this letter that I had been unwell. That is the fact, though I believe I am about well now; but that, with other things I can not account for, have conspired and have gotten my spirits so low, that I feel that I would rather be any place in the world than here. I really can not endure the thought of staying here ten weeks. Write back as soon as you get this, and if possible

*say something that will please me, for really I have not [been]*
*pleased since I left you. This letter is so dry and [stupid] that*
*I am ashamed to send it, but with my pres[ent feel]ings I can*
*not do any better. Give my respects to M[r. and] Mrs. Abell*
*and family. Your friend*

*Miss Mary S. Owens*                          *Lincoln*[52]

The second letter was written the next year from Springfield. Lincoln
was still lonely and doubtful about Mary's true feelings for him.

*Springfield, May 7, 1837*

*Friend Mary*

*I have commenced two letters to send you before this, both of*
*which displeased me before I got half done, and so I tore them*
*up. The first I thought wasn't serious enough, and the second*
*was on the other extreme. I shall send this, turn out as it may.*

*This thing of living in Springfield is rather a dull business*
*after all, at least it is so to me. I am quite as lonesome here as*
*[I] ever was anywhere in my life. I have been spoken to by but*
*one woman since I've been here, and should not have been by her,*
*if she could have avoided it. I've never been to church yet, nor*
*probably shall not be soon. I stay away because I am conscious*
*I should not know how to behave myself.*

*I am often thinking about what we said of your coming to live*
*at Springfield. I am afraid you would not be satisfied. There is*
*a great deal of flourishing about in carriages here, which it would*
*be your doom to see without shareing in it. You would have to*
*be poor with out the means of hiding your poverty. Do you*
*believe you could bear that patiently? Whatever woman may cast*
*her lot with mine should any ever do so, it is my intention to do*
*all in my power to make her happy and contented; and there is*
*nothing I can imagine, that would make me more unhappy than*

to fail in the effort. I know I should be much happier with you than the way I am, provided I saw no signs of discontent in you. What you have said to me may have been in jest, or I may have misunderstood it. If so, then let it be forgotten; if otherwise, I much wish you would think seriously before you decide. For my part I have already decided. What I have said I will most positively abide by, provided you wish it. My opinion is that you had better not do it. You have not been accustomed to hardship, and it may be more severe than you now immagine. I know you are capable of thinking correctly on any subject; and if you deliberate maturely upon this, before you decide, then I am willing to abide your decision.

You must write me a good long letter after you get this. You have nothing else to do, and though it might not seem interesting to you, after you had written it, it would be a good deal of company to me in this "busy wilderness." Tell your sister I don't want to hear any more about selling out and moving. That gives me the hypo whenever I think of it. Yours, &c,

*Lincoln.*[53]

Lincoln wrote again in late summer.

*Springfield Aug. 16th 1837*

*Friend Mary,*

You will, no doubt, think it rather strange, that I should write you a letter on the same day on which we parted; and I can only account for it by supposing, that seeing you lately makes me think of you more than usual, while at our late meeting we had but few expressions of thoughts. You must know that I can not see you, or think of you, with entire indifference; and yet it may be, that you are mistaken in regard to what my real feelings towards you are. If I knew you were not, I should not trouble you with this letter. Perhaps any other man would know enough without further information; but I consider it my peculiar right to plead ignorance, and your bounden duty to allow the plea. I want in all cases to do right, and most particularly so, in all cases with women. I want, at this particular time, more than any thing else, to do right with you and if I knew it would be doing right, as I rather suspect it would, to let you alone, I would do it. And for the purpose of making the matter as plain as possible, I now say, that you can now drop the subject, dismiss your thoughts (if you ever had any) from me forever, and leave this letter unanswered, without calling forth one accusing murmer from me. And I will even go further, and say, that if it will add any thing to your comfort, or peace of mind, to do so, it is my sincere wish that you should. Do not understand by this, that I wish to cut your acquaintance. I mean no such thing. What I do wish is, that our further acquaintance shall depend upon yourself. If such further acquaintance would contribute nothing to your happiness, I am sure it would not to mine. If you feel yourself in any degree bound to me, I am now willing to release you, provided you wish it; while, on the other hand, I am willing, and even anxious to bind you faster, if I can be convinced that it will, in any considerable degree, add to your happiness. This, indeed, is the whole question with me. Nothing would make me more miserable than to believe you miserable — nothing more happy, than to know you were so.

In what I have now said, I think I can not be misunderstood; and to make myself understood, is the only object of this letter.

If it suits you best to not answer this — farewell — a long life and a merry one attend you. But if you conclude to write back, speak as plainly as I do. There can be neither harm nor danger, in saying, to me, any thing you think, just in the manner you think it.

My respects to your sister. Your friend

Lincoln.[54]

It appears that Mary did not reply, as this is the last letter written by Lincoln to her. It is clear that he was impressed with Mary and when her sister suggested that Mary would return if Lincoln would propose to her, he agreed. When Mary returned, he was dismayed to see that she had gained quite a lot of weight during her absence. Lincoln described Mary and the situation in a later letter to Mrs. Orville Browning:

*Springfield, April 1, 1838.*

*Dear Madam:*

*Without appologising for being egotistical, I shall make the history of so much of my own life, as has elapsed since I saw you, the subject of this letter. Any by the way I now discover, that, in order to give a full and inteligible account of the things I have done and suffered since I saw you, I shall necessarily have to relate some that happened before.*

*It was, then, in the autumn of 1836, that a married lady of my acquaintance, and who was a great friend of mine, being about to pay a visit to her father and other relatives residing in Kentucky, proposed to me, that on her return she would bring a sister of hers with her, upon condition that I would engage to become her brother-in-law with all convenient dispach. I, of course, accepted the proposal; for you know I could not have done otherwise, had I really been averse to it; but privately between you and me, I was most confoundedly well pleased with the project. I had seen the said sister some three years before, thought her inteligent and agreeable, and saw no good objection to plodding life through hand in hand with her. Time passed on, the lady took her journey and in due time returned, sister in company sure enough. This stomached me a little; for it appeared to me, that her coming so readily showed that she was a trifle too willing; but on reflection it occurred to me, that she might have been prevailed on by her married sister to come, without any thing concerning me ever having been mentioned to her; and so I concluded that if no other* objection presented itself, I would consent to wave this. All this occurred upon my hearing of her arrival in the neighbourhood; for, be it remembered, I had not yet seen her, except about three years previous, as before mentioned.

In a few days we had an interview, and although I had seen her before, she did not look as my immagination had pictured her. I knew she was over-size, but she now appeared a fair match for Falstaff; I knew she was called an "old maid", and I felt no doubt of the truth of at least half of the appelation; but now, when I beheld her, I could not for my life avoid thinking of my mother; and this, not from withered features, for her skin was too full of fat, to permit its contracting in to wrinkles; but from her want of teeth, weather-beaten appearance in general, and from a kind of notion that ran in my head, that nothing could have commenced at the size of infancy, and reached her present bulk in less than thirtyfive or forty years; and, in short, I was not all pleased with her. But what could I do? I had told her sister that I would take her for better or for worse; and I made a point of honor and conscience in all things, to stick to my word, especially if others had been induced to act on it, which in this case, I doubted not they had, for I was not fairly convinced, that no other man on earth would have her, and hence the conclusion that they were bent on holding me to my bargain. Well, thought I, I have said it, and, be consequences what they may, it shall not be my fault if I fail to do it. At once I determined to consider her my wife; and this done, all my powers of discovery were put to the rack, in search of perfections in her, which might be fairly set-off against her defects. I tried to immagine she was handsome, which, but for her unfortunate corpulency, was actually true. Exclusive of this, no woman that I have seen, has a finer face. I also tried to convince myself, that the mind was much more to be valued than the person; and in this, she was not inferior, as I could discover, to any with whom I had been acquainted.

Shortly after this, without attempting to come to any positive understanding with her, I set out for Vandalia, where and when you first saw me. During my stay there, I had letters from her, which did not change my opinion of either her intellect or intention; but on the contrary, confirmed it in both.

All this while, although I was fixed "firm as the surge repelling rock" in my resolution, I found I was continually repenting the rashness, which had led me to make it. Through life, I have been in no bondage, either real or immaginary from the thraldom of which I so much desired to be free.

After my return home, I saw nothing to change my opinion of her in any particular. She was the same and so was I. I now spent my time between planing how I might get along through life after my contemplated change of circumstances should have taken place; and how I might procrastinate the evil day for a time, which I really dreaded as much — perhaps more, than an irishman does the halter.

After all my suffering upon this deeply interesting subject, here I am, wholly unexpectedly, completely out of the "scrape"; and I now want to know, if you can guess how I got out of it. Out clear in every sense of the term; no violation of word, honor or conscience. I don't believe you can guess, so I may as well tell you at once. As the lawyers say, it was done in the manner following, towit. After I had delayed the matter as long as I thought I could in honor of, which by the way had brought me round into the last fall, I concluded I might as well bring it to a consumation without further delay; and so I mustered my resolution, and made the proposal to her direct; but, shocking to relate, she answered, No. At first I supposed she did it through an affectation of modesty, which I thought but ill-become her, under the peculiar circumstances of her case; but on my renewal of the charge, I found she repeled it with greater firmness than before. I tried it again and again, but with the same success, or rather with the same want of success. I finally was forced to give it up, at which I verry unexpectedly found myself mortified almost beyond endurance. I was mortified, it seemed to me, in a hundred different ways. My vanity was deeply wounded by the *reflection, that I had so long been too stupid to discover her intentions, and at the same time never doubting that I understood them perfectly; and also, that she whom I had taught myself to believe no body else would have, had actually rejected me with all my fancied greatness; and to cap the whole, I then, for the first time, began to suspect that I was really a little in love with her. But let it all go. I'll try and out live it. Others have been made fools of by the girls; but this can never be with truth said of me. I most emphatically, in this instance, made a fool of myself. I have now come to the conclusion never again to think of marrying; and for this reason; I can never be satisfied with any one who would be block-head enough to have me.*

*When you receive this, write me a long yarn about something to amuse me. Give my respects to Mr. Browning. Your sincere friend*

*Mrs. O. H. Browning.*                                    *Lincoln*[55]

In 1841, Mary Owens married Jesse Vineyard and moved to Weston, Missouri, a proslavery town. She had five children; two of her sons fought in the Civil War for the Confederacy. She died July 4, 1877.

W. H. Herndon, Lincoln's law partner, who would later write a biography of Lincoln, wrote to Mrs. Vineyard in 1866, requesting more information about her relationship with Lincoln. She responded in part May 1, 1866:

*After quite a struggle with my feelings I have at last decided to send you the letters in my possession written by Mr. Lincoln, believing as I do that you are a gentleman of honor and will faithfully abide by all you have said. My associations with your lamented friend were in Menard County whilst visiting a sister who then resided near Petersburg. I have learned that my maiden name is now in your possession; and you have ere this, no doubt, been informed that I am a native Kentuckian.*[56]

She responded to Herndon's questions in another letter from Weston:

*Weston, Mo., May 22, 1866*

*Mr. W. H. Herndon,*

*My Dear Sir: Really, you catechise me in true lawyer style; but I feel you will have the goodness to excuse me if I decline answering all your questions in detail, being well assured that few women would have ceded as much as I have under all the circumstances.*

*You say you have heard why our acquaintance terminated as it did. I too have heard the same bit of gossip; but I never used the remark which Madame Rumor say I did to Mr. Lincoln. I think I did on one occasion say to my sister, who was very anxious for us to be married, that I thought Mr. Lincoln was deficient in those little links which make up the chain of woman's happiness — at least it was so in my case. Not that I believed it proceeded from a lack of goodness of heart; but his training had been different from mine; hence there was not that congeniality which would otherwise have existed.*

*From his own showing you perceive that his heart and hand were at my disposal; and I suppose that my feelings were not sufficiently enlisted to have the matter consummated. About the beginning of the year 1838 I left Illinois, at which time our acquaintance and correspondence ceased, without ever again being renewed.*

*My father, who resided in Green County, Kentucky, was a gentleman of considerable means; and I am persuaded that few persons placed a higher estimate on education than he did.*

*Respectfully yours,*

*Mary S. Vineyard.*[57]

She wrote Herndon again in July of that same year concerning his question about Lincoln's inconsiderateness during a certain incident. Supposedly Lincoln, Mrs. Bowlin Greene, and Mary Owens were climbing the hill to a friend's house. Mrs. Greene was carrying her child, a "fat" baby boy, and was bent under the load. Lincoln never offered to assist in the carrying of the child.

*Weston, Mo., July 22, 1866*

*Mr. W. H. Herndon:*

*Dear Sir: I do not think you are pertinacious in asking the question relative to old Mrs. Bowlin Greene, because I wish to set you right on that question. Your information, no doubt, came through my cousin, Mr. Gaines Greene, who visited us last winter. Whilst here, he was laughing at me about Mr. Lincoln, and among other things spoke about the circumstance in connection with Mrs. Greene and child. My impression is now that I tacitly admitted it, for it was a season of trouble with me, and I gave but little heed to the matter. We never had any hard feelings towards each other that I know of. On no occasion did I say to Mr. Lincoln and I did not believe he would make a kind husband, because he did not tender his services to Mrs. Greene in helping of her carry her babe. As I said to you in a former letter, I thought him lacking in smaller attentions. One circumstance presents itself just now to my mind's eye. There was a company of us going to Uncle Billy Greene's. Mr. Lincoln was riding with me, and we had a very bad branch to cross. The other gentlemen were very officious in seeing that their partners got safely over. We were behind, he riding in, never looking back to see how I got along. When I rode up beside him, I remarked, "You are a nice fellow! I suppose you did not care whether my neck was broken or not." He laughingly replied (I suppose by way of compliment), that he knew I was plenty smart to take care of myself.*

*In many things he was sensitive almost to a fault. He told me of an incident: that he was crossing a prairie one day and saw before him "a hog mired down," to use his own language. He was rather "fixed up," and he resolved that he would pass on without looking at the shoat. After he had gone by, he said the feeling was irresistible; and he had to look back, and the poor thing seemed to say wistfully, "There now, my last hope is gone"; that he deliberately got down and relieved it from its difficulty.*

*In many things we were congenial spirits. In politics we saw eye to eye, though since then we differed as widely as the South is from the North. But methinks I hear you say, "Save me from a political woman!" So say I.*

*The last message I ever received from him was about a year after we parted in Illinois. Mrs. Able visited Kentucky, and he said to her in Springfield, "Tell your sister that I think she was a great fool because she did not stay here and marry me." Characteristic of the man!*

*Respectfully yours,*

*Mary S. Vineyard.*[58]

This was certainly an interesting episode in Lincoln's life. His letters reveal a young man who was insecure with his ability to please Mary and to measure up to her qualifications for a husband. This young Lincoln is a dramatic contrast to the mature Lincoln of 1859 who was so secure in his beliefs and his ability to draw people to him.

*Chapter Six*

# The End
# of the Story

ANOTHER PERSON came to Leavenworth who would play a dramatic role
in the Abraham Lincoln story. John
Wilkes Booth arrived four years later to the month after
Lincoln's visit and appeared on the same stage, now
called the Union Theatre as of 1862. On December 22,
1863, the *Leavenworth Daily Times* reported:

> J. Wilkes Booth, arrived last night and
> tonight plays Richard III at the Union.
> Secure seats early.

The following ad appeared in the *Leavenworth Daily
Times* on December 20, 1863.

```
 A  M  U  S  E  M  E  N  T  S.
           ——
 UNION THEATRE!
 A. S. ADDIS,.............................................Proprietor.
 G. D. Chaplin,....................Acting and Stage Manager.

   Monday Evening, Dec. 21st, 1863.
                  ———
  First night of the celebrated young and talented
             American tragedian,

        J. WILKES BOOTH,
   Who will appear in his great character of Richard,
   in Shakspeare's grand Tragedy, in five acts, of

        RICHARD III;
               —OR—
 The Battle of Bosworth Field!
                  ———
   Concluding with the laughable Farce of
 YOUR LIFE'S IN DANGER.
                  ———
     Extra Notice—Change of Time
   In future doors will open at seven.  Curtain rises
 at half-past seven precisely.
                  ———
        PRICES OF ADMISSION:
 Parquette,....................................... 50 cents
 Gallery....................................... 25 cents
```

The *Daily Conservative* ran an article about Booth on December 10, 1863.

> WILKES BOOTH. — This distinguished tragedian, an hon-
> ored member of the famous family of actors, will make his first
> appearance here to-morrow night in his father's great part of
> "Richard."
> When Mr. Booth first appeared in New York, the <u>Tribune</u>
> contained a very elaborate criticism of his style of acting, and
> represented him as in many respects the most talented of the
> trio. Since that time, Wilkes Booth has played engagements in
> all our large cities, and with the most triumphant success. Mr.
> Addis has again given proof of his liberality and enterprise in

John Wilkes Booth.
*Kansas State Historical Society, Topeka*

bringing to Leavenworth an actor of the genius and power of
Wilkes Booth.

The *Daily Conservative* praised Booth again on December 20th.

RICHARD III. — Mr. Booth is here, and a rare treat awaits
those who visit the Theatre this evening. He is a born tragedian, as all must be who attain to the highest rank as actors. In
addition to his natural gifts, Mr. Booth has had the finest
instructions which Europe and America can afford. His fine
intellectuality has received those graces which enhance even

the splendors of genius, and add a charm to the most gifted natures. In seeing him, we witness an actor on whom nature and art have lavished their gifts, and who, even in his youth, has reached the highest walks of the drama.

His "Richard" is a marvellous piece of acting, and should be seen by all who would see Shakespeare translated by a true artist.

Mr. Booth's engagement in this city will be very brief.

The *Daily Conservative* called Booth's visit brief, but in a 13-day period from December 19th through December 31st, Booth appeared in an astounding seven major tragedies including *Richard III*, *Hamlet*, *Love and Pride* or *Lady of Lyons*, *The Robbers*, *Richelieu*, *Othello* — in which he played Iago — and *Raphael* — which was performed twice. Ironically, the afternoon play on December 25th, Christmas Day, was *Uncle Tom's Cabin*, the classic that exposed slavery for the evil it was. One must wonder if the Southern sympathizer Booth watched the play and how he responded.

The *Leavenworth Daily Times* on December 24, 1863, also acclaimed Booth to be a great tragedian.

J. Wilkes Booth, as a tragedian, is all he has been represented. His Richard the Third of Tuesday night, was a fine conception. We never witnessed a more thrilling representation of deceit, hate, revenge and ambition combined and intensified than in his Richard. In Hamlet, last night, he was equally good. People who love pure tragedy can be gratified at the Union during the engagement of Mr. Booth. Tonight he appears as "Claude Melnotte" in "Lady of Lyons."

At the close of the week on January 1, 1864, the *Daily Conservative* reported:

J. WILKES BOOTH. — We have enjoyed the performances of this brilliant and intellectual young artist as we have done that of no other actor who has ever visited our city, with the exception, perhaps, of Mr. Couldock. Mr. Booth closed his engagement last night by a fine rendering of Iago. A man of

# UNION THEATRE!

A. S. ADDIS,.......................................................Proprietor.
G. D. Chaplin,.............................Acting and Stage Manager.

**Thursday Evening, Dec. 31st, 1863.**

Benefit and last appearance of

## J. WILKES BOOTH,

Who will appear in his great character of IAGO, in
Shakespeare's great tragedy of

## OTHELLO,

OR THE

## MOOR OF VENICE!

Concluding with the glorious farce of the

## LIMERICK BOY!

☞ Two grand performances on New Year's Day.
Afternoon at 2, and evening at 7½ o'clock.

**Extra Notice — Change of Time**

In future doors will open at seven.    Curtain rises
at half-past seven precisely.

PRICES OF ADMISSION.

Parquette,.............................................................. 50 cents
Gallery.................................................................... 25 cents

Advertisement of John Wilkes Booth's last performance in Leavenworth,
December 31, 1863.

intellect, of high culture and attainments he has well profited by
the advantages, which combined with his striking personal
appearance, always bespeak for him a welcome. . . . We hope to
welcome Mr. Booth to our city again.

Booth returned to Washington, D.C., and 16 months later became a part
of a tragedy that would shock and sadden the world. Later, F. E. Jerome,
a stage scenery painter from Leavenworth, would recall his less-than-
enthusiastic impressions of Booth.

Recollections of J. Wilkes Booth,
In Leavenworth, Kansas,
In December, 1863.

In December, 1863, I was employed, with my brother, John
Jerome, in painting scenery in Morgan's Theater, which stood
on the southwest corner of Delaware and Fourth Streets, Leavenworth, but which was destroyed by fire a short period after
that time. Several "stars" had come and gone, and a new attraction, Miss Jean Hasmer, was filling an engagement there, when
we heard that J. Wilkes Booth "The great tragedian," had closed
an engagement with Mr. Morgan for four or five nights, I forget which. This announcement filled me with the greatest
excitement when I heard it, as also others in the theater, who
knew of his then rising fame in The Eastern States, but my
excitement was of a different nature.

Mother and father had both been well acquainted with the
Booth family, and also Benjamin DeBars, who owned the St.
Louis Opera House in 1860, 1861, and I think in 1862, who was
Wilkes' Uncle. Father made the acquaintance of the family, I
think, in Cincinnati, Ohio, and mother having told me many
anecdotes about them, I of course was extremely anxious to see
Wilkes, who I was confidential informed was a greater actor
than his brother. Childlike, I had thought these matters over in
their most rosy colors, and was prepared to see what I thought
to be a giant among other actors with whom I had become
familiar.

I think it was arranged for him to commence his engagement
on a Monday, but for some reason he failed to put in an appearance on that day, and Miss Hasmer was finally persuaded to fill
the vacancy for Monday night, which she did.

I forget the name of the play put upon the stage, but at about
the close of the second or third act, the hurried whisper went the
rounds behind the curtain that J. Wilkes Booth was in front
among the audience. While the rest were peeping from behind
the curtain, I also found a convenient hole in the canvas and
saw him for the first time. To say that my air castles "dropped"
with my "peep," is but the simple truth. I saw before me a

comparative young man of sharp piercing eyes, glossy curly hair, a pallid, dissipated face, with a soft fur cap on his head, a cigar in his mouth, his pants rolled up half way to his boot tops, sitting negligently in one of the chairs talking to Mr. Morgan, with his little shining boots stuck up over the chair in front of him. The coarseness of his habit attracted the attention of the audience, who were ladies and gentlemen of high standing in the city, and I saw many fair noses turn up in disgust as the owners looked at him and turned and whispered to each other. But he paid not the least attention to any of this, and did not take off his cap or relinguish his cigar even when the curtain rose, but leaned his head back with a half sarcastic smile, and smoked his cigar and kept his boots elevated on the seat until the curtain dropped on the last act. Miss Hasmer was justly indignant at his lack of manners, and said he "hadn't any more manners than a dog," which proved to be a very truthful saying as his after proceedings in the theater verified. The first play he took part in, was "Taming a Shrew," and I am of the opinion that he was intoxicated from the beginning to the ending of the piece. I found him behind the scenes to be devoid of gentlemanly manners of any kind, and remarks he made that made many blush and turn away, were said regardless of who there were around him, or who heard them, male or female, and he had a coarse reckless manner of throwing himself on anything else around, that those behind the scenes were kept continually dodging out of his way — in every way acting as a "bully" over small fry. As a consequence, he was cordially hated before his engagement closed, and when he left I heard more than one say "good riddance to bad baggage!"

Of course his playing on the stage partook of his natural manners, and it was crash, bang, on the stage, and when he left it, if the audience failed to cheer, he would scowl and mutter to himself about them being a set of "d—d fools." He courted praise more than anything else, but never acknowledged it. Butterflies, and you will find them everywhere, flocked around him, with flattery that I well knew they never meant, but rather for the champaigne and wines that he always had waiting for him behind the scenes, and he would take this flattery with laughable dignity, and then start to telling them of his exploits in Eastern States, and what a set of green fools these were in Kansas! His coarse jokes that made my childish mind tingle with shame and mortification only made his followers laugh louder, and say he was "deuced sharp!"

I heard him say in one of these debauches that he didn't believe in fate: "Fate takes hold of some even, but with me I do not wait for Fate; I make my own fate, and have to thank no man for it!" A saying which I found to be indeed true, when I learned that he had foully assassinated our beloved President, Abraham Lincoln, and covered his name with an odious that even that of Benedict Arnold's was an honor compared with his!

F.E. Jerome.

Russell, Kans.,
August 18, 1886.[1]

After John Wilkes Booth shot Lincoln in Ford's Theatre, he fled the Capital on horseback and sought shelter in a barn in the country. A detachment of the Sixteenth New York Cavalry, stationed near Washington, pursued Booth with orders to capture him alive. Its commander, Lieutenant Edward P. Doherty, had asked for 25 volunteers. One of the first men to volunteer was Sergeant Boston Corbett. He had been released from Andersonville prison only five months earlier through an exchange of prisoners. The Sixteenth Cavalry followed Booth, surrounded the barn, and, when Booth would not come out, set it afire. Corbett asked several times to be allowed to go into the barn and bring Booth out, but his commanders declined to allow it. Booth still refused to come out. Corbett recalls what happened next.

When Lieutenant Doherty demanded Booth's surrender, he shouted, "No!" Three times the lieutenant gave the order, three times Booth refused. The lieutenant then gave the command to fire the barn. A torch was lighted and touched to it.

In the flickering light, I could see Booth through cracks, between boards, standing on a pile of hay. He was leaning on a crutch with his carbine in hand.

As fire mounted up, he suddenly raised his carbine, I saw the move, took aim, and fired. In an instant, he crumpled on the hay.

He was dragged outside and carried to the back porch of the nearby house. He died there some time later.

I was straightaway placed under arrest for daring to disobey orders. They disarmed me and took me to Washington. There the officers treated me with scorn . . . because I shot Booth!

General Howard asked me, "How in the world did you happen to send the bullet to the same spot, exactly to the tilting of a hair, where Lincoln was shot?"

"The Lord directed it," I told him.[2]

After Booth was shot through the neck, he was pulled from the fire, but died from the gunshot wound a short time later, whispering, "Tell mother I die for my country." Corbett was charged with disobeying an order and brought before Edwin M. Stanton, Secretary of War. Stanton released Corbett saying, "The rebel is dead — the patriot lives — he has saved us continued excitement, delay and expense — the patriot is released."[3] Corbett received $1,653.85 as a reward for shooting Booth.

Boston Corbett was born Thomas Corbett in London, England, in 1832. At the age of seven, he moved with his parents to Troy, New York, where he learned the trade of hat finisher. He married, but his wife and an infant child died in childbirth in 1855, an event that seemed to have a profound effect on his life. Despondent over their death and unable to pay his debts, he took to drink.

In 1859, Corbett moved to Boston, Massachusetts, became a member of the Methodist Episcopal Church and was baptized. Because this was such a significant event in his life, he took the name "Boston" in honor of his conversion. In an attempt to free himself of sexual temptation, Boston took a pair of scissors and emasculated himself. After his recovery from his injuries in Massachusetts General Hospital, he went to New York where he continued in his religious fanaticism at the Fulton Street meetings. There he was known for praying aloud and adding "er" to all of his words — "O Lord-er, hear-er our prayer." When pleased, he would shout

Boston Corbett in 1865.
*Kansas State Historical Society, Topeka*

"Amen," or "Glory to God." At this time he also seems to have recovered from his alcoholism.[4]

While in New York, Corbett enlisted in the New York State Militia, but his religious fervor and the military life were not a good mix. The other soldiers taunted him for his constant praying and *Bible* reading, and he was in perpetual trouble. Corbett was especially sensitive to cursing and would many times drop to his knees and pray when he heard it. One day at a dress parade, Colonel Butterfield cursed the regiment for some action he disliked. Corbett stepped out of the ranks and rebuked the Colonel for breaking God's law. He was arrested and eventually put out of the regiment. After the beginning of the Civil War, there was such a need for men, that Corbett was able to re-enlist with the Sixteenth New York Cavalry. The Sixteenth was captured by Mosby's Rangers. Corbett was the last man resisting surrender, firing until he ran out of ammunition. His bravery impressed Colonel John Mosby and he ordered his men not to shoot. The captured Corbett eventually was sent to Andersonville prison in Georgia, where he remained for five months. He was an exchange prisoner at Savannah, Georgia, November 19, 1864, where he was described as a "walking skeleton" and was hospitalized at Annapolis, Maryland. At the time he shot John Wilkes Booth, he was still not fully recovered.

In August 1865, Boston Corbett was a volunteer witness at the trial of Captain Henry Wirz, the commandant of the Andersonville prison. Captain Wirz was being tried for alleged atrocities committed against Union prisoners during the war. Corbett testified that during an unseasonable spell of cold weather he had stayed warm by huddling with Wirz's hound dogs. When asked why he had not been bitten by the dogs as had the other prisoners, Corbett replied: "The same power that kept the lions from biting Daniel to pieces is the same in whom I trust."[5]

Corbett came to Kansas in 1878 and homesteaded 80 acres near Concordia, in Cloud County. Corbett was 46 years old, was small in stature, and wore a moustache and thin beard. Albert T. Reid, a young boy growing up in Concordia, described Corbett as having long hair that strayed from under his old Army cap and hung down to his shoulders. Around his waist was an Army belt, and from it dangled two pistols. Corbett lived alone in a stone-fronted dugout with a wooden floor. The structure had a fort-like appearance with small holes in the walls to view the countryside and a surrounding trench. He attended church, and would sit or stand in the back. Sometimes, at the end of the service, he would tell the minister the Lord wanted him to say a few words. Then he would take off his guns and lay them on each side of the *Bible* before he began to speak. It was the only time he would be unarmed.[6]

Corbett's only trusted companion in Kansas was his horse Billy, which he fed copious sugar cubes. Many thought he had come to Kansas to escape the publicity he received in the East as the killer of Booth. He had also supposedly received threats to avenge Booth's death. Perhaps this was why he was a loner, even remaining distant from his neighbors. He planted a cottonwood tree on a small hill, and under it dug his own grave. He showed his neighbors the Army blanket in which he wanted to be buried.

Corbett's strange behavior was accepted until one day when he threatened to shoot some neighbor children. This tried the patience of his neighbors and Corbett was arrested. The trial was recalled by Fred W. Sturges, a former district court judge who was in the room.

> There was Boston Corbett, a little slender, wary-eyed chap, his hair hanging down long behind, sitting there quietly, while these fellows told how he had threatened to shoot them. Suddenly he jumped up, whipped out his Army revolver and began pointing it at one man after another.
>
> "That's a lie, a lie, a lie," he shrilled, "I'll shoot any man who says such things about me," exclaimed Corbett.

I can tell you there was scattering. One old attorney, who was crippled up with rheumatism and knew he could not make much showing in a run, crawled under a small table. But Boston didn't shoot and nothing was done to him either. They quieted him down and talked to him and he went back to his hillside eighty, the cabin and the pony.[7]

In spite of his strange behavior, he was given a job as an assistant door-keeper in the House of Representatives at Topeka where he received much attention as the killer of Booth. One day, when angry, he threatened to shoot two employees and was taken before a judge, pronounced insane, and sent to the state asylum at Topeka. Corbett had remained there for over a year when he escaped in 1888 by riding off on a pony left tied on the asylum grounds.[8]

Flyers were sent across Kansas warning that Boston Corbett had escaped and was dangerous. Corbett fled to Neodesha, Kansas, where his friend, Richard Thatcher, lived. Thatcher, who was the superintendent of schools, had also been a prisoner at Andersonville and had been sympathetic to Corbett while in the asylum. Thatcher's daughter, who was still living at home, recalled Corbett staying with her father two days.

He was unarmed, she recalled. He took his horse to the country, tied a note to him, telling whom he belonged to, and turned him loose. That was on June 30, 1888. When he left she accompanied him and her father to the train.

She recalls hearing her father ask Corbett if he needed any money and he answered "No, I have more than enough to last me."[9]

Even though there were several reported sightings of Corbett, none had ever been verified and he was never seen again.

And so the story of Abraham Lincoln's run for the presidency that began in Kansas with his first presidential campaign speech in Leavenworth would be ended by a future Kansan in a barn outside of

# INSANE MAN ESCAPED.

TOPEKA, KANSAS, May 26, 1888.

DEAR SIR:

BOSTON CORBETT, an insane man, escaped from the Insane Asylum at Topeka this morning, and is supposed to be heading for Cloud County. He is about 55 years of age; about 5 feet, 4 inches high; has plucked all his beard out down to the lower part of his ears; has gray chin whiskers and moustache; gray hair, cut square at bottom, and parts his hair in the middle; he wore a dark jeans suit, and black soft hat; and was riding a bay or sorrel pony with a boy's saddle.

He is regarded as a dangerous man, but was unarmed when he escaped. If he comes your way arrest him and return him to the Asylum at once, or telegraph Dr. B. D. EASTMAN, Superintendent Insane Asylum, Topeka, for orders.

G. A. HURON,

Guardian BOSTON CORBETT.

Kansas State Historical Society, Topeka

Washington, D.C. The death of Abraham Lincoln was profound, not only in Kansas, but around the world. Mark Delahay may have summed up the loss of Lincoln best when he said,

> . . . Since the day of the Calvary and the Cross, perhaps no man
> will be found to have stamped upon the future a more enduring

record, or marked a grander epoch in the history of the world, than that accomplished by the simple mind, and pure heart of the murdered Lincoln.[10]

Kansas had been politically and ideologically aligned with Lincoln from the beginning, through their shared fight for Kansas to be a free state. The people of Kansas, in many instances, sacrificed their homes, their goods, and, for some, their lives, making a strong stand against slavery before it was required of them by their government. This sacrifice touched Lincoln and ensured that he and the people of Kansas would always be close. Lincoln's hold on the hearts of Kansans was obvious by their enthusiastic reception and response to his speeches and appearances. Perhaps they saw in this simple but honest man a glimpse of the future greatness he would achieve. Little did they know on that cold December day in 1859 that they had become a part of the story of the 16th President, and that together, Kansans and Abraham Lincoln would lead the way for the nation in its difficult, but successful, pilgrimage to free itself of slavery forever.

# Appendix A

### The Saint Mary Collection

**W**HEN LEAVING the four-lane highway and turning onto the brick-paved, winding lane toward Saint Mary College, one enters another world. The quiet, green meadows, tree-lined lanes, and towering Victorian spire take one back to the 19th century. But the beautiful facade belies the excitement that imbues the learning behind the walls of this small, liberal arts college.

One of the treasures of the Saint Mary College is its Lincoln Collection, housed in the De Paul Library behind the round, crossed window. The Collection boasts one of four copies of the 13th Amendment; a letter signed by Mary Todd Lincoln and the President — the only one known to exist; a telegram written to Mary from President Lincoln dated April 2, 1865 — the last he would write to his wife; a lock of Lincoln's hair clipped from his head after his death; the full set of Bernhardt Wall's *Following Abraham Lincoln* etched prints; and many other original documents signed by Lincoln. The Collection has statues, busts, coins, stamps, music, campaign buttons, original broadsides, and just about anything connected to Abraham Lincoln.

The Collection of over 10,000 items was given to the college by Dr. Bernard Hall, a Kansan, for two reasons: he wanted his collection to stay "at home" and be available to scholars and the public alike, and because Lincoln's visit to Leavenworth occurred at such a critical time in the future President's political career. Dr. Hall made the first gift in 1970, and over the years continued his donations to the library. After his death in 1987, De Paul Library received the remaining pieces. The Collection's present benefactors are Lieutenant General (Retired) and Mrs. Robert Arter.

### 13th Amendment

Abraham Lincoln's focus from the beginning of his presidency was to save the Union — a Union trying to exist half-slave and half-free. Even though he was opposed to slavery, his first duty was, above all else, to the

Part of the Lincoln Collection, Saint Mary College.

Union. Lincoln was reluctant to adopt an abolitionist policy because he feared it would impel the border slave states to join the seceded Southern states. He had also been elected on a platform pledging to leave slavery alone in the South and he doubted the constitutionality of any such interference. Lincoln once told a delegation that a Presidential Proclamation to emancipate the slaves would be as effective as "the Pope's bull against the comet." However, as the war progressed and the Union Armies continued to do poorly, Lincoln became convinced that the only way to save the Union and win the war was to emancipate the slaves. When he wrote the Emancipation Proclamation, which took effect on January 1, 1863, it really had little impact, as it only freed slaves in the Rebel states. The Proclamation did not touch slavery in any states that had not seceded from the Union. The Proclamation promised:

> . . . that on the first day of January, in the year of our Lord, one thousand-eight hundred and sixty three, all persons held as slaves within any State, or designated part of a State, the people whereof shall then be in rebellion against the United States, shall be then, thenceforth and forever free. . . .

The Saint Mary Collection boasts an original broadside of the Emancipation Proclamation, dated 1864, with "decorated borders of ornate drawings of freed negroes." Even though it was ineffective, the Emancipation Proclamation was important, in that it pointed to the event that did change slavery in the United States forever — the 13th Amendment.

The first 13th Amendment was passed in 1861 shortly after Lincoln took office, but it did not free the slaves. On the contrary, it guaranteed that slavery could never be abolished. It was passed by both houses of Congress; however, with the outbreak of the Civil War, it failed to be ratified by the states and eventually disappeared. In 1864, Lincoln's fellow Republican from Illinois, Senator Lyman Trumbull, proposed the second 13th Amendment. This Amendment abolished slavery forever and gave Congress the duty of enforcement. The Amendment required a two-thirds majority; it passed the Senate but failed the House. Lincoln, determined that the amendment must pass, did behind-the-scenes politicking — buying votes through the offer of patronage. Finally, on January 31, 1865, thirteen Democrats changed their votes and the resolution passed the House in a 119 to 56 vote.

Noah Brooks, who was present at the scene, wrote:

> For a moment there was a pause of utter silence. Then there
> was an explosion, a storm of cheers, the like of which probably
> no Congress of the United States ever heard before. Strong men
> embraced each other with tears. The galleries and aisles were
> bristling with standing, cheering crowds . . . women's handker-
> chiefs waving and floating; hands . . . shaking; . . . arms about
> each other's necks, and cheer after cheer . . . burst after burst.

Amidst the wild celebration, great guns were uncovered on Capitol Hill
and fired off into the sky, announcing to the world that "slavery was no
more."[1]

Lincoln believed the passage of the 13th Amendment to be the most
important event of his administration; some would say it was the most
important event of the 19th century. His joy was obvious when he
exclaimed upon the passage of the Amendment,

> I . . . congratulate . . . myself, the country, and the whole world
> upon this great moral victory.[2]

Lincoln's home state of Illinois was the first to ratify the Amendment,
but he did not live to see the final required ratification by three-fourths
of the states, on December 18, 1865, that made the 13th Amendment
a legal document and freed all of the slaves in the United States forever-
more.

The Lincoln Collection's 13th Amendment is one of four original
copies. It is signed by President Abraham Lincoln, Vice President Hanni-
bal Hamlin, Speaker of the House Schuyler Colfax, and 36 U.S. Senators
including the two first Kansas Senators, James H. Lane and Samuel C.
Pomeroy. The copy of the Amendment was presented by the Honorable
John P. Usher, Lincoln's Secretary of the Interior, to Governor Joseph A.
Wright of Indiana, and by Mrs. Wright to Reverend Bishop Edmund S.
Janes on January 1, 1870. Mrs. Wright probably gave the Amendment to
Bishop Janes after the death of her husband because of their strong friend-
ship and also because of Janes' connection to Lincoln. The Reverend
Janes, a Bishop of the Methodist Episcopal Church, recalls that when he
visited Lincoln during the war that they would pray together:

Many times during the war, when I visited Lincoln in his private office in Washington, he said: "Do not go, Bishop, until you have prayed with me. We need your prayers and the divine direction in these critical hours." And so, time after time, I knelt by Mr. Lincoln in the White House when we two were alone, and carried the cause of the Union and the needs of the President's anxious heart and of our distracted country to the Lord in prayer.[3]

### Letter Signed by President and Mrs. Lincoln

One of the Saint Mary Lincoln Collection's more valuable documents is a letter written by Mary Todd Lincoln to Major General John E. Wool on behalf of Mr. Thomas Stackpole. It is co-signed by President Lincoln and is the only known letter to be signed by both Mrs. Lincoln and the President. Dated July 3, 1862, the letter is written on black-bordered mourning stationery, as 11-year-old Willie, the Lincoln's third son, had died on February 20, 1862, from what was thought to be typhoid fever — possibly as a result of the contaminated White House water supply. Tad had become ill but survived.

The Lincolns had four sons. Their second son, Edward, died of tuberculosis in 1850 when he was four years old, while the Lincolns were still in Springfield. Thomas "Tad," the Lincoln's fourth son, who had a cleft palate and a lisp, died when he was 18, possibly of pneumonia. Only Robert, their eldest son, lived to adulthood. Mary was left inconsolable by each of these deaths, and took months to recover enough to return to a somewhat normal life. Even decades later she would burst into tears at the mention of one of her dead sons.

Mary Todd Lincoln's letter was sent to a Major General Wool, who was in command of the Middle Department based at Fort McHenry, Maryland.

*Soldier's Home, July 3*

*Major General Wool*

*Dear Sir:*

*Allow me to return you, my most sincere thanks, for your kindness in recommending my friend, Mr. Stackpole and any*

Soldier's Home. July.

1862

Major General Wool

Dear Sir:

Allow me to return you, my most sincere thanks, for your kindness in recommending my friend, Mr Stackpole and any further service you can render him, will be duly appreciated by the President & myself. We are very anxious to have our friend have the place as Sutler, to the School of Instruction, to oblige him and any thing, you can do to forward it

This page and next: Lincoln's original letter to Major General Wool.

further service you can render him, will be duly appreciated by the
President & myself. We are very anxious to have our friend have
the place as Sutler, to the School of Instruction, to oblige him
and any thing, you can do to forward it will be pleasantly remembered.

    With kindest regards I remain,

                        Very respectfully

                        Mrs. Lincoln
                        A. Lincoln

    As Mr. Stackpole is visiting Baltimore, I take the liberty
of sending you a bouquet.

Mary Todd Lincoln.

*Kansas State Historical Society, Topeka*

Evidently, Mary's letter was disregarded by Major General Wool, as she wrote another to him about the same position for Thomas Stackpole on September 30, 1862. A subsequent letter from Mary, dated January 15, 1864, was sent to a General Benjamin F. Butler requesting that a now-commissioned Captain Stackpole be given a permit to go into the oyster trade.

The presidency weighed so heavily on Abraham Lincoln that time spent with his wife and family was greatly impacted. After 18 years of marriage, in which Mary had been Lincoln's confidant and supporter in all things, including politics, it was very difficult for her to be left out of his sched-ule. Mary said herself that some days she only saw him briefly at the end of the day. Bereft of her husband's company and grieving severely for her son, Mary Todd Lincoln turned to others around her for companionship and comfort. Unfortunately, some of these people took advantage of Mrs. Lincoln for their own purposes. Stackpole, a watchman at the White House — some sources call him a "guard" or "engineer" — was evident-ly one of these persons. Mrs. Lincoln brought him into her confidences, as she did many of the people who served her. She seemed to have had exten-sive communication and contact with Stackpole. Justin and Linda Turner's book, *Mary Todd Lincoln: Her Life and Letters*,[4] includes the Saint Mary Collection's letter along with the rest of Mary's correspondence. Mary referred to Stackpole in 18 other letters and sent him 1 telegram. While the early letters were recommendations for Stackpole, many of the later letters were about Stackpole's indebtedness to the Lincolns for $360, which had not been repaid.

The Lincolns were socially ostracized in Washington, and Mary suf-fered especially. In an attempt to overcome her country-bumpkin label and gain acceptance, she decided to redecorate the White House, and spent $27,000 in the process. Lincoln was very distressed when he saw the bill and furiously declared;

> It can never have my approval — I'll pay it out of my own pocket first — it would stink in the nostrils of the American people to have it said that the President of the United States had approved a bill over-running an appropriation of $20,000 for

flub dubs — for this damned old house, when the soldiers cannot have blankets.[5]

Mary Todd Lincoln certainly was, by all accounts, a difficult person, and her penchant for overspending was well known. She was very emotional and erratic in her behavior; but when the events that preceded this letter are understood, one feels a certain empathy for Mary and the difficult times she lived through in the White House.

### The Telegram — The Last Written Note to Lincoln's Wife

One of the Saint Mary Collection's most interesting documents is a telegram dated April 2, 1865, 8:15 p.m., written from City Point, Virginia, by Abraham Lincoln to his wife Mary. Lincoln and his son Tad had gone out to City Point, General Ulysses S. Grant's headquarters, to be close to the battlefield. Lincoln liked to be near the battle to give advice and stay up-to-date on the current state of the war. The handwritten telegram, on General Grant's official stationery, includes "Mrs. A. Lincoln, Washington D.C." at the top. Lincoln reported:

> At 4:40 p.m. to-day, Gen. Grant telegraphs that he has Petersburg completely enveloped from river below, to river above, and has captured, since they started last Wednesday, about twelve thousand prisoners and fifty guns.

To Lincoln, the imminent fall of Petersburg, Virginia, spelled the end of the war and the end of bloodshed. The receipt of the glorious news must have moved him deeply. His thoughts turned simultaneously to his wife and to his Commanding General. To Grant, at 8:15 p.m., he wired, ". . . the Nation's grateful thanks for this . . . magnificent success." To Mrs. Lincoln, at the identical hour, he reported Grant's news, and that

> He suggests that I shall go out and see him in the morning, which I think I will do.

He added a personal note:

> Tad and I are both well, and will be glad to see you and your party here at the time you name.

It is the last written message Lincoln ever penned to his wife.

This is a wonderful document because it is the coming together of many of the elements of Lincoln's life: he is writing as the President, as a husband, and as a father. He speaks of General Grant, of the fall of Petersburg, and the end of the war. When one considers what a burden the war had been to Lincoln, politically and personally, one can understand what a relief it must have been to him to know the end was near.

From the beginning, the war went poorly for the Union. Battles were being lost and Lincoln could not find a General who would fight as aggressively as he wanted. When Lincoln received a telegram telling of the terrible defeat of the Union Army at the Battle of Chancellorsville, May 2 to 4, 1863, with a loss of over 16,000 Union soldiers — the Confederacy lost 12,000 and General Thomas J. "Stonewall" Jackson — he burst into tears and cried, "My God, My God, what will the country say?"[6] That night Lincoln's secretary, William O. Stoddard, staying late to clear out the tremendous backlog of mail, could hear the tread of the President's feet as he strode back and forth in his study all through the night. Almost fearful of what he would find in the morning, Stoddard entered the President's room to find him eating breakfast.

Lincoln had agonized all night whether to end the war, as so many men were dying, or to press on and try to win a battle. By morning he had written the order to General Joseph Hooker to push forward and to fight again. The next battle would be Gettysburg and as he later told General Daniel E. Sickles,

> . . . I went to my room one day, and locked the door, and got down on my knees before Almighty God, and prayed to him mightily for victory at Gettysburg. I told him that this was his war, and our cause his cause, but we couldn't stand another Fredericksburg or Chancellorsville, and I then and there made a solemn vow to Almighty God, that if he would stand by our boys at Gettysburg, I would stand by him. And he did stand by you boys, and I will stand by him. And after that (I don't know how it was, and I can't explain it), soon a sweet comfort crept into my soul that God Almighty had taken the whole business into his own hands and that things would go all right at Gettysburg. And that is why I had no fears about you.[7]

*Saint Mary College Collection*

The Army of the Potomac fought a desperate battle at Gettysburg, but maybe no more desperate than that already fought by its leader on his knees through long nights of torment. This was the burden lifted from his shoulders on that day of April 2, 1865, by the telegram from the General who had won the war for him. This was the news that he had to share with his wife.

Tad had become a source of comfort for Lincoln after the death of Willie. He alone could cheer Lincoln in the most difficult times, and this was the Tad that he wrote about in his last message to his wife. This document speaks volumes about Abraham Lincoln's life: the war, his perseverance, his devotion to his family, his pride in his General, his faith in God, and the final outcome of the war.

## Lincoln Letter

As is true of many of the documents in the Saint Mary Collection, the letter to Colonel James B. Fry, the Provost Marshal General, from Abraham Lincoln, seems rather cut-and-dried unless one knows the story behind it. Lincoln asks the Provost Marshal to

> *. . . see and hear the Mayor of this City about the draft, in this District, and come to an agreement with him if you consistently can, and if you can not, then get the point, or points, of difference distinctly stated, so that I can see and understand them.*

The letter, dated April 12, 1864, is referring to the controversial Enrollment Act — also called Conscription — passed in March 1863.

When Fort Sumter, South Carolina, was fired upon in April 1861, Lincoln called upon the Governors of the states to furnish 75,000 militia for three-months service to suppress what was thought to be a short-term rebellion. The Northern states responded enthusiastically, sending more troops than was required. The Border states, however, were not so enthusiastic. Missouri, Kentucky, Maryland, and Delaware found their loyalties were divided between a desire to support the Union or the seceded South. Unfortunately, the Border states lay in the path of the troops from the Northern states as they marched to Washington. When the Massachusetts Sixth Regiment attempted to pass through Baltimore, they were confronted by a mob who disputed their passage. The fervent Massachusetts Sixth responded by firing into the mob, killing nine people. By the time the Sixth had fought its way to the Washington train, its men were carrying the corpses of four of their own.[8] Just about the time the fighting cooled down, General Benjamin F. Butler, commanding more Massachusetts troops, arrived by boat at Annapolis, Maryland, and was advised not to land his troops. The intrepid General not only landed his troops and seized the railroad, but offered to President Lincoln "to bag the whole nest of traitorous Maryland legislators."[9]

The troops, identified by their states, were under the authority of their Governors, who raised the troops, organized them into regiments, housed, fed, and clothed them, and sent them to Washington. Governor John A. Andrew of Massachusetts raised his troops so quickly and efficiently, that as he was giving his parting benediction to the troops, ". . . tailors worked furiously between the ranks, sewing the last buttons on the tails of the men's overcoats."[10] When the troops arrived in Washington, D.C., they

Executive Mansion,

Washington, April 12, 1864.

Provost. Marshal. General.

My dear Sir

Please see and hear the Mayor of this City about the draft, in this District, and come to an agreement with him if your consistently can, and if you can not, then get the point, or points, of difference distinctly stated, so that I can the more understand them,

Yours truly

A. Lincoln

found a War Department unprepared to house, arm, or financially support them — a War Department that was unorganized and inefficient. Not only was Secretary of War Simon Cameron not up to the task, but there was confusion as to who was in charge of the troops, the states or the national government. Lincoln quickly saw the difficulty of the situation and in May when he called for more troops to serve, they were called for three years or the duration of the war and were to be subject to the regulations governing the Army of the United States. Lincoln had become Commander-in-Chief of the military.

The states began to have increasing difficulty meeting their troop requirements. The number of volunteers slowed tremendously, due to the inefficiency of the War Department in paying the troops, and a population that was largely composed of farmers who did not want to commit themselves to three years of service. With the Union doing poorly in the war and men being induced to join up by bounties, desertions became a problem. Some regiments dwindled to as few as 35 men. In an effort to overcome all of these difficulties, Congress passed the Enrollment Act in March 1863, giving the Provost Marshals the right to enroll all men aged 20 to 45 in their districts. Exemptions were offered to men who paid $300 or who provided a substitute.[11]

The Enrollment Act was not received enthusiastically. Indeed, the Provost Marshals attempting to enforce the Act were met with great resistance, and in some cases were forced to take a posse with them for protection. Anti-Draft riots in New York City had to be quelled by troops.

When it was found that black substitutes would be accepted in place of drafted white men, there was a rush by several free states to complete their quotas by enlisting blacks from the Border states and the District of Columbia.[12]

Conscription became a seriously discussed topic in Washington. In early August 1863, a blind man had drawn the names from a wheel in the courtroom at the City Hall. One-third of the men drafted were blacks.

Southern sympathizers and government employees were not exempt. A clerk in the War Department committed suicide when he learned he had been drafted.[13] The Draft procured 960, of whom 675 were paid substitutes, still far short of the District's quota of 3,863 soldiers. Although the government bounty had been raised to $300 and $400, a Washington committee worked diligently through the winter to solicit funds to supplement the bounty and entice more volunteers.

President Lincoln called for more volunteers in the fall and again in the winter. When no quota had been assigned to the District of Columbia by February 1, 1864, Mayor Richard Wallach wrote Provost Marshal General Fry inquiring the reason. The entire district quota, including all former calls, was more than 12,000 men. Wallach considered the quota excessive and wanted it based on the census of 1860 rather than Washington's greatly increased wartime population. He was eventually successful and the quota was changed.

### A Lock of Lincoln's Hair

The Saint Mary Lincoln Collection contains a lock of Lincoln's hair clipped from his head at the time of his death. It is placed over a small engraving of Lincoln in a daguerreotype case (shown on the front cover of this book). The provenance of the hair is traced in the following history, which is signed at the bottom by R. Gerald McMurtry, the man from whom Dr. Bernard Hall purchased the hair in 1966.

One of the largest and finest collections of Lincolniana was acquired over a long period of years by the late Oliver R. Barrett (1873-1950) of Chicago, Illinois. The story of his great private collection was written by Carl Sandburg and was published in a 344-page book by Harcourt, Brace and Company in 1950. On page 208 of this book Sandburg described among other things, "A small box with three locks of hair . . ." which was one of the prized possessions of the collector.

On February 19th and 20th of 1952 the Barrett collection was sold at an auction in the Parke-Bernet Galleries, Inc., 908 Madison Avenue, New York, New York. An illustrated catalogue of the collection was published and on page 84, item 155 listed "Locks of Hair. Abraham and William Lincoln. Small box with three locks of hair, inscribed: No. 1. Willie Lincoln's hair, No.2. Abraham Lincoln's hair taken from his head after death, No. 3. Abraham Lincoln's hair clipped from his head at the tomb."

Item No. 155 was sold to Glenn Blodgett who retained the relics from 1952 until 1966. In April, 1966, C.W. Loud, Route # 1, Petersburg, Illinois, purchased from the widow of the late Glenn Blodgett the three locks of hair in the original box for re-sale at his auction on Sunday, November 27, 1966. The hair was sold in the original box from the Parke-Bernet Sale of the Barrett Estate in 1952. Also included in this lot is a fine Gutta Percha frame, opening size 4″ x 5½″ which would be perfect for mounting these rare items." The estimated value of the lot was $450.00.

The locks of hair were purchased at the auction by James T. Hickey, Curator of the Lincoln Collection of the Illinois State Historical Library, Springfield, Illinois and R. Gerald McMurtry, Director of the Lincoln National Life Foundation, Fort Wayne, Indiana on Wednesday, November 17, 1966. On December 6, 1966, the locks of hair were photographed in the original box and then divided equally by R. Gerald McMurtry between the two owners; each receiving a half portion of the hair contained in the three different locks. From these original locks the owners will make up smaller locks of hair for distribution and re-sale.

Knowing Lincoln's wonderful sense of humor, one would guess he would get a chuckle considering that people would actually want to buy and portion out his hair. One can be sure that the request of a Miss Jennings in 1864 for a lock of his hair gave Lincoln an opportunity for merriment. It had become expected that each year the "Sanitary Fairs," the fund raising source for the United States Sanitary Commission — the Civil War version of the Red Cross — would solicit contributions from the President to raise funds for wounded soldiers. Given Lincoln's intense desire to help the soldiers, it was almost impossible for him to refuse any request. In 1863, the ladies conducting the fair asked for the original copy of the Emancipation Proclamation. Lincoln was hesitant, being aware of the far-reaching influence of the paper, and was reluctant to part with it. As he said,

> I had some desire to retain the paper; but if it shall contribute to the relief or comfort of the soldiers that will be better.[14]

This request was followed the next year by a request for the Gettysburg Address. Then it was suggested that Lincoln should write small autographed notes while he was listening to the requests of prospective office holders. That way his time could be better employed and the ladies' fund-raiser would be the benefactor of these otherwise wasted minutes of the President. These notes would then be donated to the cause.

Lincoln must have felt at this point that the ladies had stepped over the boundaries of the ridiculous, only to be astounded by their next request. This note was received from a Miss Jennings on January 22, 1864:

> *I am desirous to obtain a lock of your hair and also some from the heads of various members of your cabinet.*[15]

It is impossible to imagine Lincoln reading this note without hearing his loud guffaws. One can hardly imagine a President, with his many other duties and concerns during the Civil War, not to mention the time he was expected to spend writing autographed notes, entering the hallowed halls of the government, scissors in hand, to snip from the august heads of his cabinet members locks of their hair. A certain difficulty would occur when he approached the toupee of Secretary Gideon Welles. Should he clip a substitute piece from the Secretary's beard or chance the possible anger of a man who has just had his expensive, European-imported toupee permanently snipped? One would think that the possibility of making such a decision would have had Lincoln "down on the floor" as they say, kicking his long legs in the air as he rolled around in uncontrolled laughter. But Miss Jennings did not stop with the cabinet; she also wanted the President to retrieve specimens of hair from "other prominent and distinguished men of the day."[16] One would assume that she would give the President full discretion in determining who those "prominent and distinguished men" were, as long as he was willing to carry out the "dirty deed." It is truly amazing that Lincoln did not proclaim a Presidential decree that all members of the cabinet and other prominent and distinguished men would be required, out of a duty to their government and in the interest of the limited time of their Chief Executive, to forthwith shave their heads and serve the rest of their terms bald.

### Bernhardt Wall, *Following Abraham Lincoln 1809-1865*

The 85-volume work, *Following Abraham Lincoln 1809-1865*, is one of the most beautiful and amazing items contained in the Saint Mary Lincoln Collection. The work is etched and printed by artist Bernhardt Wall, who spent 11 years following the footsteps of Lincoln, making the etchings of famous Lincoln landmarks in all parts of the country.

The books are small, 7½-inch by 8½-inch boards, with etched titles, published in Lime Rock, Connecticut, as a serial publication between 1931 and 1942. This is a sumptuous work, printed in various colors, direct from the etched plates. It is comprised of 1,040 hand-printed pages of which 530 are views of buildings and the like, historically connected with Abraham Lincoln's life. Each of the 530 plates are signed by the artist. The published edition was limited to 100 sets; only 36 were completed. Each volume bears a signed inscription in Wall's hand, "To R. Gerald McMurtry, Esq. Sincerely Bernhardt Wall."

Bernhardt Wall was born in Buffalo, New York, on December 30, 1872. He began his career as a lithograph artist in 1889. By 1920, after having served in World War I, Wall had published his first all-etched book. His style of tracing superbly executed portraits and inscriptions onto copper plates with an engraving needle and acid would be used to publish many books and periodicals. His method was unique in that rather than the usual letterpress Wall printed each page by hand from an etched plate, including the text as well as illustrations.

After publishing his *World War Etchings*, Wall began the first all-etched periodical in the history of art, *Wall's Etched Monthly*. *Following Abraham Lincoln* was the crowning event in his professional life. In 1943, Bernhardt was awarded a Doctorate of Humane Letters by Lincoln Memorial University, in Harrogate, Tennessee, for his outstanding work in the field of Lincolniana. He also published miniature books about Lincoln entitled *Abraham Lincoln's Chronology* and *Lincoln's Gettysburg Speech*, of which the De Paul Library at Saint Mary College has a copy. Appropriately, the man who became known as the nation's foremost etcher and who spent much of his career etching the history of Abraham Lincoln, died on February 9, 1956, and was buried on Lincoln's birthday.

   The Saint Mary Lincoln Collection was a gift from Dr. Bernard Hall to the world, but particularly to Kansans in recognition of the importance of Lincoln's visit to our state. It stands as a memorial to Dr. Hall's respect and admiration for Abraham Lincoln and as a reminder of the important place in history held by Lincoln and Kansas in the struggle to abolish slavery. Saint Mary College is grateful for the gift from Dr. Hall and eager to

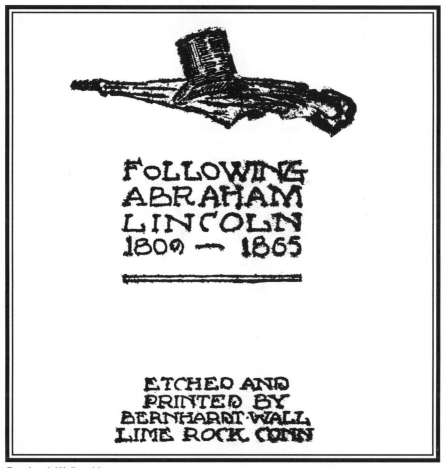

Bernhardt Wall etching.                                    *Saint Mary College Collection*

Methodist Church, Atchison, Kansas, in which Lincoln spoke on **Dec. 2, 1859.** Collection, Kansas State Historical Society, Topeka

Lincoln's first speech in Kansas was delivered at Elwood, Dec. 1, 1859. The next on Dec. 2 at Troy. Lincoln was brought in a buggy, arriving blue with cold. Spoke at Doniphan, Atchison and Leavenworth.

Buggy owned by Henry Bayer, Esq, Leavenworth

Massasoit House, Atchison, Kansas, where Lincoln stopt on Dec. 2, 1859. Horace Greeley also stopt here in 1859. Collection of Kansas State Historical Society, Topeka

Bernhardt Wall etchings.

*Saint Mary College Collection*

Planters Hotel, Leavenworth, Kansas, where Lincoln entertained the Kansans with stories Dec. 4, 1859.

carry out his wish to share it. The Collection is available for viewing by appointment with the Special Collections Librarian, De Paul Library, Saint Mary College, Leavenworth, Kansas.

# Appendix B

**Synopsis of Lincoln's**
**December 3, 1859, Speech in Leavenworth**[1]

*T*HE *Kansas Historical Collection* has the most complete reproduction of Lincoln's Leavenworth speech. Lincoln had not made a complete copy of the presentation. After being introduced to the large audience by Colonel Mark W. Delahay, Abraham Lincoln said, substantially as follows:

"Ladies and Gentlemen: You are, as yet, the people of a territory; but you probably soon will be the people of a state of the Union. Then you will be in possession of new privileges, and new ideas will be upon you. You will have to bear a part in all that pertains to the administration of the national government. That government from the beginning has had, has now and must continue to have a policy in relation to domestic slavery. It cannot, if it would, be without a policy upon that subject; and must, of necessity, take one of two directions. It must deal with the institution as being wrong, or as not being wrong."

Mr. Lincoln then stated, somewhat in detail, the early action of the general government upon the question — in relation to the foreign slave trade, the basis of federal representation, and the prohibition of slavery in the federal territories; the fugitive-slave clause in the constitution — and insisted that, plainly, that early policy was based on the idea of slavery being wrong; and tolerating it so far, and only so far, as the necessity of its actual presence required.

He then took up the policy of the Kansas-Nebraska act, which he argued was based on opposite ideas — that is, the idea that slavery is not wrong. He said: "You, the people of Kansas, furnish the example of the first application of this new policy. At the end of about five years, after having almost continual struggles, fire, and bloodshed, over this very question, and after having framed several state constitutions, you have, at last, secured a free-state constitution under which you will probably be admitted into the Union. You have at last, at the end of all this difficulty, attained what we, in the old Northwest Territory, attained without any difficulty at all. Compare, or rather contrast, the actual working of this new policy with that of the old, and say whether, after all, the old way — the way adopted by Washington and his compeers — was not the better."

Mr. Lincoln argued that the new policy had proven false to all its promises — that its promise to the nation was to speedily end the slavery agitation, which it had not done, but directly the contrary — that its promises to the people of the territories was to give them greater control of their own affairs than the people of former territories had had; while, by the actual experiment, they had had less control of their own affairs and had been more bedeviled by outside interference than the people of any other territory ever had been. He insisted that it was deceitful in its expressed wish to confer additional privileges upon the people; else it would have conferred upon them the privilege of choosing their own officers; that if there be any just reason why all the privileges of a state should not be conferred on the people of a territory at once, it only could be the smallness of numbers; and that if, while their number was small, they were fit to do some things, and unfit to do others, it could only be because those they were unfit to do were the larger and more important things; that, in this case, the allowing the people of Kansas to plant their soil with slavery, and not allowing them to choose their own governor, could only be justified on the idea that the planting a new state with slavery was a very small matter, and the election of governor a very much greater matter. "Now . . . compare these two matters and decide which is really the greater. You have already had, I think, five governors, and yet, although their doings, in their respective days, were of some little interest to you, it is doubtful whether you now even remember the names of half of them. They are gone (all but the last) without leaving a trace upon your soil, or having done a single act which can, in the least degree, help or hurt you, in all the indefinite future before you. This is the size of the governor question.

"Now, how is it with the slavery question? If your first settlers had so far decided in favor of slavery as to have got 5000 slaves planted on your soil, you could, by no moral possibility, have adopted a free-state constitution. Their owners would be influential voters among you, as good men as the rest of you, and, by their greater wealth and consequent greater capacity to assist the more needy, perhaps the most influential among you. You could not wish to destroy or injuriously interfere with their property. You would not know what to do with the slaves after you had made them free. You would not wish to keep them as underlings; nor yet to elevate them to social and political equality. You could not send them away. The slave states would not let you send them there, and the free states would not let you send them there. All the rest of your property would not pay for sending them to Liberia. In one word, you could not make a free state if the first half of your own numbers had got 5000 slaves fixed upon the soil. You could have disposed of, not merely five, but 500 governors easier. There they would have stuck, in spite of you, to plague you and your children, and your children's children indefinitely. Which is the greater, this, or the governor question? Which could the more safely be entrusted to the first few people who settle a territory? Is it that which, at most, can be but temporary and brief in its effects, or that which, being done by the first few, can scarcely ever be undone by the succeeding many?"

He insisted that, little as was popular sovereignty at first, the Dred Scott decision, which is indorsed by the author of popular sovereignty, has reduced it to still smaller proportions, if it has not entirely crushed it out. That, in fact, all it lacks of being crushed out entirely by that decision is the lawyer's technical distinction between decision and dictum. That the court has already said a territorial government cannot exclude slavery; but, because they did not say it in a case where a territorial government had tried to exclude slavery, the lawyers hold that saying of the court to be dictum and not decision. "But," said Mr. Lincoln, "is it not certain that the court will make a decision of it the first time a territorial government tries to exclude slavery?" Mr. Lincoln argued that the doctrine of popular sovereignty, carried out, renews the African slave trade. Said he: "Who can show that one people have a better right to carry slaves to where they have never been than any people have to buy slaves wherever they please, even in Africa?"

He also argued that the advocates of popular sovereignty, by their efforts to brutalize the negro in the public mind — denying him any share in the declaration of independence, and comparing him to the crocodile — were beyond what avowed proslavery men ever do, and really did as much, or more than they, toward making the institution national and perpetual.

He said many of the popular-sovereignty advocates were as much opposed to slavery as any one, but that they could never find any proper time or place to oppose it. In their view, it must not be opposed in politics, because that is agitation; nor in the pulpit, because it is not religion; nor in the free states, because it is not here; nor in the slave states, because it is there. These gentlemen are never offended by hearing slavery supported in any of these places. Still, they are "much opposed to slavery as anybody."

One would suppose that it would exactly suit them if the people of the slave states should themselves adopt emancipation; but when Frank Blair tried this last year, in Missouri, as was beaten, every one of them threw up his hat and shouted "Hurrah for democracy!" Mr. Lincoln argued that those who thought slavery right ought to unite on a policy which should deal with it as being right; that they should go for a revival of the slave trade; for carrying the institution everywhere, into free states as well as territories; and for a surrender of fugitive slaves in Canada or war with Great Britain. Said he: "All shades of democracy, popular sovereign as well as the rest, are fully agreed that slaves are property and only property. If Canada now had as many horses as she has slaves belonging to Americans, I should think it just cause of war if she did not surrender them on demand. On the other hand, all those who believe slavery wrong should unite on a policy dealing with it as wrong. They should be deluded into no deceitful contrivances, pretending indifference, but really working for that to which they are opposed." He urged this at considerable length.

He then took up some of the objections to republicans. They were accused of being sectional. He denied it. What was the proof? "Why, they have no existence, get no votes in the South. But that depends on the South, and not on us. It is their volition, not ours; and if there be fault in it, it is primarily theirs, and remains so unless they show that we repel them by some wrong principle. If they attempt this, they will find us holding no principle other than those held and acted upon by the men who gave us the government under which we live. They will find that the charge of sectionalism will not stop at us, but will extend to the very men who gave us the liberty we enjoy. But if the mere fact that we get no votes in the slave states makes us sectional, whenever we shall get votes in those states we shall cease to be sectional; and we are sure to get votes, and, a good many of them, too, in these states next year. You claim that you are conservative, and we are not. We deny it. What is conservatism? Preserving the old against the new. And yet you are conservative in struggling for the new and we are destructive in trying to maintain the old. Possibly you mean that you are conservative in trying to maintain the existing institution of slavery. Very well; we are not trying to destroy it. The peace of society and the structure of our government both require that we should let it alone, and we insist on letting it alone.

"If I might advise my republican friends here, I would say to them, Leave your Missouri neighbors alone. Have nothing whatever to do with their slaves. Have nothing whatever to do with the white people, save in a friendly way. Drop past differences, and so conduct yourselves that, if you cannot be at peace with them, the fault shall be wholly theirs.

"You say that we have made the question more prominent than heretofore. We deny it. It is more prominent; but we did not make it so. Despite of us, you would have a change of policy; we resist the change, and, in the struggle, the greater prominence is given to the question. Who is responsible for that, you or we? If you would have the question reduced to its old proportions, go back to the old policy. That will effect it. But you are for the Union; and you greatly fear the success of the republicans would destroy the Union. Why? Do the republicans declare against the Union? Nothing like it. Your own statement of it is, that if the black republicans elect a president you won't stand it. You will break up the Union. That will be your act, not ours. To justify it, you must show that our policy gives you just cause for such desperate action. Can you do that? When you attempt it, you will find that our policy is exactly the policy of the men who made the Union. Nothing more and nothing less. Do you really think you are justified to break up the government rather than have it administered by Washington and other good and great men who made it, and first administered it? If you do, you are very unreasonable; and more reasonable men cannot and will not submit to you. While you elect the president, we submit, neither breaking nor attempting to break up the Union. If we shall constitutionally elect a president, it will be our duty to see that you submit. Old John Brown has just been executed for treason against a state. We cannot object, even though he agreed with us in thinking slavery wrong. That cannot excuse violence, bloodshed, and treason. It could avail him nothing that he might think himself right. So, if constitutionally we elect a president, and therefore you undertake to destroy the Union, it will be our duty to deal with you as old John Brown has been dealt with. We shall try to do our duty. We hope and believe that in no section will a majority so act as to render such extreme measures necessary."

Mr. Lincoln closed by an appeal to all, opponents as well as friends, to think soberly and maturely, and never fail to cast their vote, insisting that it was not a privilege only, but a duty to do so. Mr. Lincoln here concluded, amid loud and long cheers. The immense crowd remained motionless for a long time to look upon the old, war-worn veteran of free-state principles. Truly never did a man win the affections of an audience so completely as did Mr. Lincoln on Saturday night.

# Notes

## CHAPTER ONE

1. Albert Castel, "The Bloodiest Man in American History," *Kansas Revisited: Historical Images and Perspectives*, ed. by Paul K. Stuewe (Lawrence: University of Kansas, 1991), 107.
2. William E. Connelley, *History of Kansas: State and People, Vol. 1* (New York: American Historical Society, Inc., 1928), 373-374.
3. Noble L. Prentis, *Kansas Miscellanies* (Topeka: Kansas Publishing House, 1889), 112.
4. *Ibid.*, 111-112.
5. *Ibid.*, 112.
6. *Ibid.*, 111.
7. Donald Gilmore, "Revenge in Kansas, 1863," *History Today*, 43 (1992): 48.
8. Dudley Taylor Cornish, "Kansas Negro Regiments in the Civil War," *Kansas Historical Quarterly*, XX (1952-1953): 420.
9. John Speer, *Life of Gen. James H. Lane: "The Liberator of Kansas"* (Garden City, KS: John Speer, Printer, 1896), 262.

10. Jay Monaghan, *Civil War on the Western Border, 1854-1865* (Lincoln: University of Nebraska Press, 1955), 303.
11. Prentis, *Kansas Miscellanies*, 104.
12. *The Capital Commonwealth*, Topeka, Kansas, December 23, 1888 (X).
13. "The Times of War and Reconstruction: Reminiscences by Hon. S. C. Pomeroy," in *Kansas Biographical Scrap Book, P, Vol. VI*, 145.
14. Speer, *Life of Gen. James H. Lane*, 234.
15. "The Times of War and Reconstruction," 143.
16. *Leavenworth Daily Times*, April 26, 1861.
17. John G. Nicolay and John Hay, *Abraham Lincoln: A History, Vol. 4* (New York: The Century Co., 1890), 107.
18. *The Kansas State Journal*, Lawrence, May 9, 1861.
19. *Leavenworth Conservative*, April 18, 1861; referenced in Edgar Langsdorf, "Jim Lane and the Frontier Guard," *Kansas Historical Quarterly*, IX, 1 (February 1940): 17.
20. *Lawrence Republican*, May 9, 1861; referenced in Edgar Langsdorf, "Jim Lane and the Frontier Guard," *Kansas Historical Quarterly*, IX, 1 (February 1940): 20-21.
21. "The Times of War and Reconstruction," 143-144.
22. Charles Robinson, *The Kansas Conflict* (New York: Harper & Brothers, Franklin Square, 1892), 456.
23. William O. Stoddard, *Lincoln's Third Secretary: The Memoirs of William O. Stoddard* (New York: Exposition Press, 1955), 211-212.
24. Speer, *Life of Gen. James H. Lane*, 281-282.
25. Monaghan, *Civil War on the Western Border*, 304.
26. Wendell Holmes Stephenson, *The Political Career of General James H. Lane* (Topeka: Kansas State Historical Society, 1930), 73.
27. Nicolay and Hay, *Abraham Lincoln*, 55.
28. Sister Mary Buckner, *History of the Sisters of Charity of Leavenworth, Kansas* (Kansas City: Hudson-Kimberly Publishing Company, 1898), 74.
29. *Ibid.*
30. Speer, *Life of Gen. James H. Lane*, 313-314.
31. Albert Castel, *The Presidency of Andrew Johnson* (Lawrence: The Regents Press of Kansas, 1979), 188.
32. Prentis, *Kansas Miscellanies*, 116.
33. John P. Burch, *Charles W. Quantrell* (Vega, TX: J. P. Burch, 1923), 19-21. (Told by Captain Harrison Trow. The same incident is in the memoirs of John McCorkle, *Three Years with Quantrell: A True Story*.)
34. Castel, "The Bloodiest Man in American History," 110.
35. *Ibid.*
36. *Ibid.*, 108.
37. *Ibid.*, 114.

38. John O. Shea, *Reminiscences of Quantrell's Raid Upon the City of Lawrence, Kas.* (Kansas City, MO: Isaac P. Moore, Printer and Binder, 1879), 24-26.
39. William E. Connelley, *Quantrill and the Border Wars* (Cedar Rapids, IA: The Torch Press, 1910; 1992), 465; Monaghan, *Civil War on the Western Border*, 346.
40. Stephen Z. Starr, *Jennison's Jayhawkers* (Baton Rouge: Louisiana State University Press, 1973), 27.
41. *Ibid.*
42. *Ibid.*, 32.
43. *Ibid.*, 257.
44. *Ibid.*, 382.
45. *Ibid.*, 386.

## CHAPTER TWO

1. William E. Connelley, *History of Kansas: State and People, Vol. 1* (New York: American Historical Society, Inc., 1928), 415.
2. *Ibid.*, 297.
3. *Ibid.*, 377.
4. *Ibid.*, 378.
5. Jay Monaghan, *Civil War on the Western Border, 1854-1865* (Lincoln: University of Nebraska Press, 1955), 11.
6. Albert Jeremiah Beveridge, *Abraham Lincoln, 1809-1858* (New York: Houghton Mifflin Company, 1928), 312-313.
7. *Ibid.*, 313.
8. Abraham Lincoln, *The Collected Works of Abraham Lincoln, Vol. II, 1848-1858*, ed. by Roy P. Basler (New Brunswick, CT: Rutgers University Press, 1953), 320-323.
9. Monaghan, *Civil War on the Western Border*, 40.
10. *Ibid.*, 54.
11. *Ibid.*, 55.
12. *Ibid.*
13. Thomas Goodrich, *War to the Knife: Bleeding Kansas, 1854-1861* (Mechanicsburg, PA: Stackpole Books, 1998), 120.
14. Connelley, *History of Kansas, Vol. 1*, 410-411.
15. *History of the State of Kansas* (Chicago, IL: A. T. Andrews, 1883), 136-137.
16. Wendell Holmes Stephenson, *The Political Career of General James H. Lane* (Topeka: Kansas State Historical Society, 1930), 73.
17. William E. Connelley, "The Lane Trail," *Kansas Historical Collections*, XIII (1913-1914): 268-279.
18. Connelley, *History of Kansas, Vol. 2*, 605.
19. Lincoln, *The Collected Works of Abraham Lincoln, Vol. II*, 452-453.

20. James G. Blaine, *Twenty Years of Congress: From Lincoln to Garfield* (Norwich, CT: The Henry Bill Publishing Company, 1884), 139.
21. Connelley, *History of Kansas State and People, Vol. 11*, 990.
22. *Ibid.*
23. Lincoln, *The Collected Works of Abraham Lincoln, Vol. IV, 1860-1861*, 241-242.

## CHAPTER THREE

1. Mark Delahay, in Robert Todd Lincoln Collection, Library of Congress, Washington, D.C.
2. Abraham Lincoln, *The Collected Works of Abraham Lincoln, Vol. III, 1858-1860*, ed. by Roy P. Basler (New Brunswick, CT: Rutgers University Press, 1953), 371-372.
3. Delahay, Robert Todd Lincoln Collection.
4. Lincoln, *The Collected Works of Abraham Lincoln, Vol. IV, 1860-1861*, 378-379.
5. Martha B. Caldwell, "When Horace Greeley Visited Kansas in 1859," *Kansas Historical Quarterly*, IX, 2 (May 1940): 122.
6. Delahay, Robert Todd Lincoln Collection.
7. Mary Delahay, "Judge Mark W. Delahay," *Kansas Historical Collection*, XX (1907-1908): 638.
8. Delahay, Robert Todd Lincoln Collection.
9. *Ibid.*
10. *Ibid.*
11. Carl Sandburg, *Abraham Lincoln: The Prairie Years — II, Vol. Two* (New York: Charles Scribner's Sons, 1926), 286.
12. Philip B. Kunhardt, Jr., Philip B. Kunhardt, III, and Peter W. Kunhardt, *Lincoln: An Illustrated Biography* (New York: Alfred A. Knopf, 1992), 8.
13. Keith W. Jennison, *The Humorous Mr. Lincoln* (New York: Bonanza Books, 1965), 46.
14. Lincoln, *The Collected Works of Abraham Lincoln, Vol. IV*, 130.
15. *Ibid.*, 129.
16. Fred Trump, *Lincoln's Little Girl* (Honesdale, PA: Boyds Mills Press, 1977), 70-72.
17. "Lincoln in Kansas," *Transactions of the Kansas State Historical Society*, VII (1901-1902): 536.
18. D. W. Wilder's Report, July 4, 1884, Kansas Historical Society Papers.
19. *The Saint Joseph Telegraph*, Thursday, August 20, 1998.
20. "Lincoln in Kansas," 536-537.
21. Henry Villard, *Lincoln on the Eve of '61: A Journalist's Story by Henry Villard*, ed. by Harold G. Villard and Oswald Garrison Villard (New York: Alfred A. Knopf, 1941), 8-9.

22. *Ibid.*
23. *The Kansas Chief*, December 3, 1959.
24. Albert D. Richardson, *The Secret Service, The Field, The Dungeon, and The Escape* (Hartford, CT: American Publishing Company, 1865), 313-315.
25. *The Kansas Chief*, December 3, 1959.
26. P. L. Gray, *Gray's Doniphan County History* (Bendena, KS: The Roycroft Press, 1905), 17.
27. *Ibid.*, 12.
28. *Atchison Globe*, December 8, 1927.
29. *Topeka Capitol*, June 1901.
30. *Atchison Globe*, February 12, 1914.
31. *Ibid.*
32. Horace Greeley, "An Overland Journey," *New York Daily Tribune*, June 1, 1859, 18-19.
33. *Atchison Globe*, February 12, 1914.
34. Lincoln, *The Collected Works of Abraham Lincoln, Vol. VII, 1863-1864*, 338.
35. Franklin G. Adams, "Reminiscences of Franklin G. Adams," *Transactions of the Kansas State Historical Society*, VII (1901-1902): 539-540.
36. *Kansas City Star*, June 26, 1890.
37. Timothy Miller, "The Recreation of Abraham Lincoln: Billiards Enthusiast or Myth Maker?," 1996. (Paper presented to the Illinois History Symposium, Annual Conference of the Illinois State Historical Society, Springfield, December 6-8, 1996.)
38. Greeley, "An Overland Journey," 23-25.

## CHAPTER FOUR

1. Martha B. Caldwell, "When Horace Greeley Visited Kansas in 1859," *Kansas Historical Quarterly*, IX, 2 (May 1940): 126.
2. *Ibid.*
3. *Leavenworth Daily Times*, December 5, 1859, 3.
4. Abraham Lincoln, *The Collected Works of Abraham Lincoln, Vol. III, 1858-1860*, ed. by Roy P. Basler (New Brunswick, CT: Rutgers University Press, 1953), 497-502.
5. *Ibid.*, 522.
6. *New York Daily Tribune*, Thursday, August 30, 1860, 6.
7. Noah Brooks, *Abraham Lincoln and the Downfall of American Slavery* (New York: G. P. Putnam's Sons, 1888; 1913), 186-187.
8. *Leavenworth Weekly Herald*, December 10, 1859, taken from *Kansas Historical Quarterly*, XX (1951-1953): 530-532.
9. L. L. Jones, in Robert Todd Lincoln Collection, Library of Congress, Washington, D.C.

10. Lincoln, *The Collected Works of Abraham Lincoln, Vol. III,* 504-505.
11. *New York Daily Tribune,* Thursday, August 30, 1860, 6.
12. *Leavenworth Weekly Herald,* December 10, 1859, taken from *Kansas Historical Quarterly,* XX (1951-1953): 530-532.
13. Cecil Howes, "Pistol-Packin' Pencil Pushers," *Kansas Historical Quarterly,* XIII (1944-1945): 116.
14. *Ibid.,* 120.
15. *Ibid.,* 116.
16. Jay Monaghan, *Civil War on the Western Border, 1854-1865* (Lincoln: University of Nebraska Press, 1955), 94.
17. Howes, "Pistol-Packin' Pencil Pushers," 119.
18. Monaghan, *Civil War on the Western Border,* 350.
19. Stephen Z. Starr, *Jennison's Jayhawkers* (Baton Rouge: Louisiana State University Press, 1973), 126.
20. *Ibid.,* 380-381.
21. Monaghan, *Civil War on the Western Border,* 350.
22. "Interview by Col. Daniel R. Anthony, in the Kansas City Star, February 23, 1902," *Transactions of the Kansas State Historical Society,* VII (1901-1902): 540-541.
23. William E. Connelley, *A Standard History of Kansas and Kansans* (New York: Lewis Publishing Company, 1918), 699.
24. Fred W. Brinkerhoff, "Address of the President: The Kansas Tour of Lincoln the Candidate," *Kansas Historical Quarterly,* XIII, 5 (1945): 294-307.
25. Robert A. Taft, "A Century of Kansas History: Abraham Lincoln in Kansas," *Kansas Teacher,* 63, 6 (February 1955): 40.
26. "Editorial item, Springfield State Journal, Saturday, December 10, 1859." *Transactions of the Kansas State Historical Society,* VII (1901-1902): 551-552.
27. *New York Daily Tribune,* Thursday, August 30, 1860, 6.

## CHAPTER FIVE

1. Mary E. Delahay, "When I Knew Lincoln," *National Historical Magazine,* 75, 2 (February, 1941): 30.
2. Mary E. Delahay, "Judge Mark W. Delahay," *Kansas Historical Collection,* X (1907-1908): 641. It appears that Mary's memoirs have a few memory mistakes. When Mary relates the mouse story she says it happened in 1864 in Baltimore and Willie was the son who removed the boot. If it was 1864, Willie was already dead. If it was 1860, the Lincolns didn't go to the convention. She also said that General Lane was at their house when Lincoln was there, but according to General Lane in early 1860 he had not met Lincoln. Mary claims that her father presented Lincoln's name at the Chicago convention and "that it fairly rocked the wigwam." If she meant

nominated she was mistaken unless Delahay nominated Lincoln at some of the peripheral meetings that happened at the convention.

3. Delahay, "When I Knew Lincoln," 31.
4. *Ibid.*, 25.
5. David Dary, "When Abe Lincoln Spoke in Kansas," *Kansas City Star Magazine*, December 12, 1976, 62.
6. Delahay, "When I Knew Lincoln," 31.
7. Julia Cody Goodman, "Julia Cody Goodman's Memoirs of Buffalo Bill," *Kansas Historical Quarterly*, XXVIII (1962): 487.
8. William F. Cody, *Life and Adventures of "Buffalo Bill"* (New York: Willey Book Company, 1927), 22-24.
9. William F. Cody, *Buffalo Bill's Own Story of His Life and Deeds* (John R. Stanton, 1917), 88.
10. *Ibid.*, 89.
11. *Ibid.*, 90-91.
12. *Ibid.*, 93-94.
13. *Ibid.*, 307.
14. Delahay, "Judge Mark W. Delahay," 640.
15. Delahay, "When I Knew Lincoln," 32-33.
16. *Tonganoxie Mirror*, February 11, 1971.
17. D. P. Hougland, "Voting for Lincoln in Missouri in 1860," *Kansas State Historical Collections*, IX (1905-1906): 518.
18. Delahay, "Judge Mark W. Delahay," 639.
19. Abraham Lincoln, *The Collected Works of Abraham Lincoln, Vol. II, 1848-1858*, ed. by Roy P. Basler (New Brunswick, CT: Rutgers University Press, 1953), 340-341.
20. *Ibid.*, 341.
21. Delahay, "Judge Mark W. Delahay," 640.
22. James H. Lane, in Robert Todd Lincoln Collection, Library of Congress, Washington, D.C.
23. William E. Connelley, *James Henry Lane: The "Grim Chieftain" of Kansas* (Topeka, KS: Crane & Company, Publishers, 1899), 109. (Speer says Lane only walked back to Lawrence and Connelley says he took a buggy.)
24. John Speer, *Life of Gen. James H. Lane: "The Liberator of Kansas"* (Garden City, KS: John Speer, Printer, 1896), 224-225.
25. *Ibid.*, 108.
26. Harry J. Carman and Reinhard H. Luthin, *Lincoln and the Patronage* (Gloucester: Peter Smith, 1964), 118.
27. *Ibid.*
28. George Templar, "Federal Judiciary of Kansas," *Kansas Historical Quarterly, XXXVIII*, 1 (1971): 4.
29. Carman and Luthin, *Lincoln and the Patronage*, 118.
30. Lincoln, *The Collected Works of Abraham Lincoln*, 31-32.

31. *Ibid.*, 44.
32. John G. Clark, "Delahay: Peripatetic Politician," *Kansas Historical Quarterly*, XXV, 3 (Autumn 1959): 302.
33. Delahay, "Judge Mark W. Delahay," 641.
34. Lincoln, *The Collected Works of Abraham Lincoln, Vol. IV*, 283.
35. Mark W. Delahay, *Abraham Lincoln* (New York: Daniel H. Newhall, 1939), unpaged.
36. Dorothy Melland, "Impeachment Fires Torched Kansas Century," *Hutchinson News*, July 21, 1974.
37. *Civil War Times,* May 1982, 30.
38. A. F. Callahan, "Leavenworth Laconics," *Daily Kansas State Journal* (January 15, 1880): 4.
39. Glenn V. Sherwood, *Labor of Love: The Life and Art of Vinnie Ream* (Hygiene, CO: Sunshine Press Publications, Inc., 1997), 9-10.
40. *Ibid.*, 94; Albert Castel, *The Presidency of Andrew Johnson* (Lawrence: The Regents Press of Kansas, 1979), 191.
41. Claude G. Bowers, *The Tragic Era: The Revolution After Lincoln* (Cambridge, MA: Houghton Mifflin Company, 1929), 195.
42. Sherwood, *Labor of Love*, 98.
43. *Ibid.*
44. Castel, *The Presidency of Andrew Johnson,* 192.
45. "Two Strangely Associated Names Embalmed in Reconstruction History," *Kansas City Star*, November 7, 1929.
46. William Tecumseh Sherman, *Memoirs of Gen. W. T. Sherman, Written by Himself, Vol. 1* (New York: Charles L. Webster & Co, 1891), 168-171.
47. *Ibid.*, 195-196.
48. *Ibid., Vol. 2*, 327-328
49. Joan Ferris Curran, *Descendant of Salomon Bloch of Janowitz, Bohemia and Baruch Wollman of Kempen-in-Posen, Prussia* (Kansas City: Gateway Press, Inc., 1996), 115.
50. William E. Connelley, *History of Kansas State and People, Vol. 1* (New York: The American Historical Society, Inc., 1928), 387, 530.
51. Curran, *Descendant of Salomon Bloch*, 118.
52. Lincoln, *The Collected Works of Abraham Lincoln, Vol. I, 1824-1828*, 54-55.
53. *Ibid.*, 78-79.
54. *Ibid.*, 94-95.
55. *Ibid.*, 117-119.
56. William H. Herndon and Jesse W. Weik, *Herndon's Life of Lincoln* (New York: World Publishing Company, 1949), 119.
57. *Ibid.*, 119-120.
58. *Ibid.*, 120-121.

## CHAPTER SIX

1. F. E. Jerome, Paper in the Kansas Historical Society.
2. David Dary. "Patriot or Madman?" *Kansas City Star Magazine*, March 12, 1972, 12.
3. *Ibid.*
4. John Redjinski, Curator of Menninger Foundation Museum, Topeka, Kansas, Paper on Boston Corbett, nd, 2.
5. *Ibid.*, 7.
6. *Ibid.*, 16.
7. *Ibid.*, 15-16.
8. *Ibid.*, 16.
9. *Topeka Capital-Journal*, November 30, 1958.
10. Mark W. Delahay, *Abraham Lincoln* (New York: Daniel H. Newhall, 1939), unpaged.


## APPENDIX A

1. Philip B. Kunhardt, Jr., Philip B. Kunhardt, III, and Peter W. Kunhardt, *Lincoln: An Illustrated Biography* (New York: Alfred A. Knopf, 1992), 270.
2. *Ibid.*, 271.
3. William J. Johnstone, *How Lincoln Prayed* (New York: Abingdon Press, 1931), 69-70.
4. Justin G. Turner and Linda Levitt Turner, *Mary Todd Lincoln: Her Life and Letters* (New York: Alfred A. Knopf, 1972), 129.
5. Kunhardt, Jr., Kunhardt, III, and Kunhardt, *Lincoln*, 284.
6. Johnstone, *How Lincoln Prayed*, 52.
7. *Ibid.*, 60-61.
8. William B. Hesseltine, *Lincoln and the War Governors* (New York: Alfred A. Knopf, 1955), 155.
9. *Ibid.*, 156.
10. *Ibid.*, 149.
11. *Ibid.*, 292.
12. Noah Brooks, *Washington in Lincoln's Time* (New York: Rinehart and Company, 1958), 104.
13. Margaret Leech, *Reveille in Washington 1860-1865* (New York: Harper & Brothers Publishers, 1941), 271.
14. *Lincoln Lore*, No. 1, 1095 (Fort Wayne, IN: Lincoln National Life Insurance Company, April 3, 1950).
15. *Ibid.*
16. *Ibid.*

# APPENDIX B

1. "Synopsis of Lincoln's Speech at Leavenworth, December 3, 1859," *Kansas Historical Collection*, 7 (1901-1902): 540-544.

# Index

## by Lori L. Daniel